THE
POVERTY
WALL

THE
POVERTY
WALL

IAN ADAMS

McClelland and Stewart Limited
TORONTO/ MONTREAL

The Canadian Publishers
McClelland and Stewart Limited
25 Hollinger Road, Toronto 374

Printed and bound in Canada

Contents

FOREWORD

When I first thought of writing a book like this, I was talking to a Newfoundland miner, who, at the age of forty-four, was diseased and dying in poverty–despite the fact that he had been a hard-working man all his life. He is the Jack Fitzpatrick whom I have written about here. Talking to him, I realized that in all probability his children would also live and die in poverty. As I finished this book in the summer of 1969, the Toronto newspapers reported that the school-board trustees of North York had spent $74,000 in a series of farewell dinners for the borough's director of education, a man earning $35,000 a year. I don't know of two better examples to illustrate the distance between the working poor and the affluent 10 per cent of the population that is the upper middle class. Apparently unaware of the gulf that exists, and pure in their own eyes, they continue to lavish money upon themselves in pursuit of status, power, and privilege.

This book is dedicated to Charlie Wenjack, who was poor and an Ojibway, two heavy strikes against anyone in our country. Charlie Wenjack found them insurmountable. I have written here how he died beside the c.n.r. mainline from exposure and starvation on the night of October 22, 1966, while attempting to walk 400 miles home to his father. He was twelve years old.

IAN ADAMS

THE
POVERTY
WALL

❧ 1 ❧

The Small Worlds of Poverty

I have been poor for most of my life, and, when I was younger, it seemed at times that I almost consciously pursued the realities of poverty. On the bum in Europe and Canada, I have woken up in jail cells to see the fleas jumping off the walls, leaping away from the bloody smears left by lice popped under the fingernail of a previous transient. I have slept on those twenty-five-cent-a-night mattresses in Montreal flophouses and lived for weeks on end in dollar-a-day Vancouver rooming houses where the transoms were made of chicken wire. I remember a landlord telling me that the chicken wire made it easier to check on any destitute roomer who might have attempted suicide.

I started working for a living before I turned sixteen, and, since then, I have left behind countless hours of my life in heavy menial labour and various mind-numbing industrial jobs. I mention all these things because I believe they are, in a way, my credentials for writing about poverty in this country. To find out how the poor live and work was not a "project" for me: by my early twenties, the bitterest years of my own poverty, I understood only too well where I stood in society. By that time, my experiences had seeped like dye into my consciousness, indelibly colouring my thoughts.

Later, as I slowly acquired the skills of a journalist, I came to understand something else: that in this country journalism is for the most part in the hands of the middle class, that much of the reporting that is done is based on the prejudices of that class. In working for daily newspapers and writing for almost every magazine in Canada, I have encountered nothing to make me change my mind. In fact, I have become convinced that for the most part my colleagues are writing for and about a world enjoyed by very few people in this country: to work for magazines is to run head-on against the values of that middle-class world. I can remember story-meetings at *Maclean's*, Canada's "national" magazine, where I was shouted down by the other staff writers when I suggested that because one-third of our citizens lived in poverty, it would be good reporting to devote a series of articles to the problem. One of the editors at that time expressed the view of the staff when he said, "Poor people are Mr. and Mrs. Welfare. They're ugly and dirty. We don't want pictures of women without teeth depressing our readers."

The same editor once seriously suggested to me that I go out and write a series about the world of real work. I reminded him that I had recently shown him an article about the effect on a man of mindless, menial drudgery. He brushed it aside. "Yes, but that's acrimonious writing. What I want is a rediscovery of the virtues of earning your living by the sweat of your brow, a reaffirmation of the joys of honest labour." Needless to say, he had never had to work that way himself.

But as every poor person knows, you don't have to be inside the system to watch the ignorance and the prejudices of the affluent in action; they are just as easily observed from the outside. In 1958, I was attending day classes at the University of Manitoba Art School. At night, from midnight to

8 A.M., I worked as a desk clerk at the Mall Hotel. In those days it wasn't quite as flossy a place as it is now, and running the hotel during those hours was a one-man affair. I checked in guests, ran the switchboard, carried luggage, delivered ice, and, when the cleaning man had a night off or was too stoned to do his work, I washed and polished the floor of the lobby. When I first went to work there, the owner often reminded me that it was a great responsibility to be so young and left in charge of the $3-million building. In turn, I would always wonder why he couldn't afford to pay me more than $50 a week.

As that winter wore on, the lack of sleep started to catch up with me, and, to keep awake during the long grey hours of the morning, I took to doing my reading while standing up at the reception counter. About 4 A.M. one morning, a drunken guest stumbled in and demanded his key. As I reached for it, his eye caught the title of the book I had been reading. It was Gaetano Mosca's theory, *The Ruling Class;* for some reason, it enraged him. "Goddamn communist bastard!" he screamed, throwing the book at my head and climbing over the counter, throwing punches and kicking. The porter and I finally overpowered him and took him up to his room, where he immediately passed out on the bed.

I learned later that the man was a well-to-do chartered accountant and was considered an important guest by the hotel management. The incident is not without its comic aspect, of course, and I describe it here because it was typical of many experiences I encountered while working there. The hotel catered to a middle-class milieu of professionals and businessmen. The head clerk liked to think of the hotel as "respectable" and described his work as "serving the public." But I found working there only degrading, and I came to the conclusion that to serve that one exclusive part of society was

13

only to have dirt heaped on my head. I left in the spring when it became apparent the hotel management was going to fire the old porter and have me do his work as well as mine. I went back to the place only once, a couple of years later; during a bleak and hungry winter, I intended to ask for the job of washing out the beer parlours after closing time. But when I saw the tired old men who desperately needed work, the heart went out of me, and I walked out without applying for the job.

My perspectives on poverty in this country have not been confined to the cities. Long before I became a journalist, I travelled this country the hard way, hitch-hiking from coast to coast four times. Twice I made the journey in winter. On the road on one such trip in north-western Ontario, near a little town called Marathon, I met two men who wanted to kill me for the coat I was wearing. They were in a bad way; they were seven weeks out of Vancouver and hadn't had a ride for five days. It was easy to understand why. They were hungry and incredibly dirty, and no driver in his right mind would pick them up. In the brief violence that ensued, my coat was torn, but I kept it, and, in doing so, I learned much about myself. I remember running down the road, half-angry, half-ashamed that I would kick another man in the stomach because he wanted my coat. But it was the only one I had. I looked over my shoulder to see if they were chasing me. One man was still crouched in the snow beside the highway; the other was shouting, waving his arms wildly. I stopped to hear what he was yelling. He wanted to know if I had any food. As if to pay for the self-knowledge I had gained, I took the three chocolate bars out of my pocket and laid them on the lonesome black road with a two-dollar bill. We stared at each other for a minute over the fifty yards that separated us, and then I turned around and kept going.

I believe it was during those years that I learned that poverty is in reality a small world, its boundaries defined by day-to-day confrontations with frustration, bitterness, and deprivation. These encounters are the daily reminders to the poor of the barriers between them and the larger world of affluence. And because there are no leaders for the poor, because there is no brotherhood of the poor, because the poor have no consciousness of themselves as a class, poverty is really thousands, millions of small worlds clustered around and upon each other like the cells of festering tissue, each cell inhabited by one of the poor—a man, a woman, or a child.

When poisonous cellular tissue is unchecked, untreated, it feeds rapidly, even voraciously, upon the healthy body. It quickly invades the veins and other visceral pathways, and soon the limb where the infection began becomes evil-smelling, gangrenous.

The poverty that poisons Canadian society aroused politicians at the beginning of 1969 to a new, if belated, awareness. But even before the year was half over, that awareness had been blunted, cut down, shaped by political and bureaucratic perspectives. The debate was no longer about the cure, about how to solve poverty, but over the degree of infection: how many poor are there in this country—6.6 million or 4.7 million?

Ironically, the economic distance that separates those two estimates is the additional income of $500 a year, a little less than $10 more a week. Only a bureaucrat could argue that an increase of $10 weekly can free an individual or a family from the fetters of poverty. (The argument is echoed in the United States where, with the War on Poverty hopelessly stalemated by politics, statisticians are debating whether there are 32 million or 50 million poor.)

The argument arose in this country in 1968, when the

Economic Council of Canada, in an attempt to establish the cut-off point at which poverty ends and affluence begins, published two sets of figures in its *Fifth Annual Review* of the nation's economy. The figures are computed on the basis of Dominion Bureau of Statistics' studies and figures gleaned from the 1961 census – it apparently takes the statisticians that long to sort out the numbers.

The E.C.C.'s conservative estimate, which sets the number of poor at 4.7 million (29 per cent of the total population), is based on the assumption that any family which has to spend 70 per cent of its income on the basics of food, clothing, and shelter is living in a condition of penury almost impossible to escape. The incomes of the families and individuals that fell into this group were classified this way: single persons with incomes below $1,500 a year; families of two with less than $2,500; and families of three, four, and five or more with incomes of less than $3,000, $3,500, and $4,000 respectively.

The second, higher estimate of 6.6 million is arrived at by saying that any family which has to spend at least 60 per cent of its income on the basic necessities of life is living in impoverished circumstances. This 10 per cent reduction raises the cut-off lines to $2,000 a year for a single person, $3,500 for a family of two, $4,000 for families of three and four, and $5,000 for families of five or more. This estimate establishes the population of the poor at about 6.6 million – without even taking low-income farm families into account.

Anyone who has worked and attempted to maintain a family can see that the income figures in the second estimate are not generous; they seem even less generous when one considers that John Porter, the Carleton University sociologist, used basically the same 1961 D.B.S. sources in establishing that *real* middle-class life only *begins* at an income of $8,000 a year. In November, 1969, the Canadian Labour Congress produced a report showing that, because of inflation, an urban family of four needed a minimum of $11,000 a year to make ends meet. During the first half of 1969, the average weekly wage in manufacturing was $110.64 a week–$5,723 a year.

However, just to be on the safe side, the E.C.C. backtracked a little more by saying, "The statement that at least one Canadian in every five suffers from poverty does not appear to be a wild exaggeration."

The marshalling of these figures and statements should not be interpreted as an attempt to discredit the E.C.C.; after all, it was only with the publication, in 1968, of its *Fifth Annual Review* that the Council made poverty "official" in Canada. It then became fashionable for publications such as *Investor Review* to devote a few sententious paragraphs to the "roaring silence" of poverty before going on to discuss investment in corporation bonds–a major source of income for less than 2.5 per cent of the 6,276,579 who filed income tax returns in 1965.

If anything, the E.C.C.'s one-in-five figure is a wildly conservative exaggeration. The table below shows how the total (non-farm) family income was shared before taxes in 1951, 1961, and 1965.

FAMILIES BY FIFTHS	DISTRIBUTION OF TOTAL INCOME			AVERAGE INCOME PER FAMILY
	1951	1961	1965	1965
lowest	6.1%	6.6%	6.7%	$ 2,263
2nd	12.9	13.4	13.4	4,542
3rd	17.4	18.2	18.0	6,102
4th	22.5	23.4	23.5	7,942
highest	41.1	38.4	38.4	13,016

17

It is immediately obvious that there has been no appreciable change of income distribution over the past fifteen years. In 1951, the lowest fifth of families had only 6.1 per cent of the total personal income, and the highest fifth had 41.1 per cent. Closer examination reveals the fact that during the fifteen-year period, the income share of Canada's neediest citizens crept at a snail's pace, up six-tenths of one per cent. Between 1961 and 1965, the increase was one-tenth of one per cent, an increase in family income from $2,083 to $2,263 before taxes. Take into account the rise in the cost of living during those fifteen years, and it is obvious that, in reality, the position of the families on the lowest rung in Canadian society has steadily deteriorated since 1951. This economic slippage is proportionately applicable to the lower three-fifths of families, those who earn $6,000 a year and less. And if you take the $8,000-a-year figure of 1961 as the point where idealized middle-class Canadian life begins—remember that numerous briefs to the Hellyer Task Force on housing proved it was impossible for a family earning less than $8,000 to afford an N.H.A. mortgage—then you are confronted with the inescapable conclusion that in 1965 more than 60 per cent of Canada's families lived *below* the economic level where middle-class life begins. Surely this explodes the myth that Canada is a "generally affluent," middle-class country, as it was described in a *Maclean's* editorial in August, 1969. It also reveals the intellectual bankruptcy of certain responsible politicians in their gropings for solutions to poverty. For example, in February, 1969, Ontario's Minister of Revenue, John White, told the Progressive Conservative Student's Association at Osgoode Hall Law School that Canada's annual welfare budget was $4 billion. He suggested that this should be redistributed so that 1 million Canadians would be guaranteed an income of $4,000 a year.

It's hard to believe that the minister didn't know that only about $600 million of the "welfare budget" is being spent to support poverty-stricken families. The $4 billion figure included old-age and war veterans' pensions, family allowances, and allowances for the crippled; a sizable chunk of the balance goes into operating and development grants for hospitals across the country. But even if it were possible to redistribute the $4 billion in the manner the minister outlined, it would not support even a quarter of the poor, who number, by the most conservative estimate, at least 4.7 million.

Poverty, as the poor well know, is a political football that is glibly tossed around in the most absurd ways. It is interesting to note that at the meeting at Osgoode Hall, Revenue Minister White refused to answer any questions. And besides, as the E.C.C. report shows, politicians and sociologists who define poverty by income statistics alone reveal only one side of the definition of poverty.

At first analysis, surveys done by the Dominion Bureau of Statistics on low-income families tend to produce a stereotyped picture of the poor; for example, you are more likely to be poor than well-off if your family is described by one or more of these characteristics:

1. The head of the family has no more than an elementary school education.
2. The family lives in a rural area.
3. The family lives in the Atlantic Provinces.
4. The head of the family is not working.
5. No member of the family worked during the year.
6. The head of the family is sixty-five or older.
7. The head of the family is a woman.

Take any two or more of these characteristics in combination, and the family is likely to *stay* poor. There is also the probability that the children of such families will in turn inherit the low standard of living and the low standard of education of their parents, reinforcing and expanding the vicious circle that is poverty. By the most conservative of E.C.C. estimates, there are at least 2 million children under sixteen who have no future but poverty.

But on the whole, these are probably the traditional ingredients of poverty: lack of education, unemployment, missing male head of the family. They are by no means the whole picture, however, only the most crippling characteristics; the following facts give a more surprising and perhaps clearer profile of poverty in this country.

Historically, the corner-stone of Canadian poverty has lain in the Atlantic Provinces, but those provinces do not contain all the poor in Canada—more than 80 per cent of all low-income, non-farm families live elsewhere than the Atlantic Provinces. Just over half live in Ontario and the Western Provinces. More than 60 per cent live in urban areas, and half of those urban residents live in the largest metropolitan cities. This is undoubtedly related to the fact that 80 per cent of Canada's manufacturing industry is located between Hamilton and Quebec City; pockets of urban poverty are sprinkled heavily throughout this industrial concentration.

Even more startling is the fact that in 1961 more than 75 per cent of low-income families had one or more wage-earners in the family—the cliché that the poor do not want to work is only another myth. Seventy-seven per cent of the family heads in the group were under sixty-five, and 87 per cent of the families were headed by men, each fact violating another accepted myth.

On the subject of myths, Herbert Marcuse, neo-Marxist and annointed prophet of the youthful rebels of our time, has written that our society's principles of freedom, individuality, and progress are commendable—the problem is that we have always been willing to sacrifice these principles to defend property and the status quo. If you look at how we have tried to deal with poverty over the years, Marcuse's criticism holds true. And Marcuse is indirectly supported when the Economic Council of Canada states, "Differences in both the levels of economic and social well-being and in economic opportunity among the various regions and provinces of Canada have persisted with only modest change for over forty years." The last four decades, in other words, have witnessed the inability of the Canadian government to provide its citizens with a more equitable distribution of the nation's wealth. And it is undoubtedly because of its political impotence that the federal government's solutions for poverty have always failed.

The most recent example of this was admitted in February, 1969, by Jean Marchand, Minister of Redevelopment, who said that more than a billion dollars had been spent since 1961 on A.R.D.A., F.R.E.D., and other programs designed to combat poverty. Almost half, some $500 million, was spent in the Atlantic region. "Unfortunately," said Marchand, "we spent money uselessly, and often we spent money too thinly over too large a territory."

Those departments whose responsibility it was to overcome poverty have now all been brought under Marchand's newly formed ministry, R.E.E.D. (Regional Economic Expansion Department). The plan of Marchand's attack on poverty is based on subsidizing industries: up to 25 per cent of capital costs and up to $5,000 for each new job to a maximum plant subsidy of $12 million. The emphasis now, he says, is going to be on centralization. This means there will be a drive to expand and encourage industrial growth in existing centres, like Halifax, St. John's, and Quebec City. The government apparently is recognizing the exodus from the nation's rural areas as inevitable, but it is now attempting to divert the people to their own regional centres, rather than letting them converge on Toronto and Montreal. But Marchand has yet to reveal his reason for assuming that industry will re-locate in these areas when it has refused to do so for the past forty years. It is simple to use public money to provide short-term employment but the disasters that have already taken place in Newfoundland and New Brunswick show the pitfalls of subsidizing new industry in areas where there is no wide industrial base. The probability is that the poor will be forced into even more miserable accommodations as the competition for adequate housing in the cities increases. It is more expensive to build a house in St. John's than in Toronto, where the Toronto Real-Estate Board reveals that inflation has pushed the price of a building lot from $5,000 to $12,000-plus in the past five years.

The Task Force on Housing, headed by Transport Minister Paul Hellyer, proposed some long overdue innovations: government land banks, a standardization of building codes, and a cutting of the snarling red tape that proliferates between levels of government and paralyses construction. Unfortunately, achieving these ends requires legislative and political machinery which the government will not be able to obtain for four or five more years. The improvement of housing conditions for the poor is obviously even further away than that. One of the few specifics that could be readily applied was the suggestion that the term of N.H.A. mortgages be increased to forty years. Unfortunately, simple mathematics reveal that this would only keep the poor in debt for a longer period of time. Richard H. Steacy, a Toronto real-estate broker, demonstrated the failings of this proposal when

22

he showed that a $10,000 mortgage loan, computed at 10 per cent over forty years, would cost $39,998.40, $8,941.20 more than a thirty-year mortgage. The difference in monthly payments would be $2.94.

As the E.C.C. points out, few programs to overcome the conditions of poverty ever really have any effect on the lives of the poor. Somehow, government measures are usually sidetracked into spending money on those income levels above the poor so that results are more quickly apparent and politically advantageous. But the struggle for political advantage is the weakest part of any government attack on poverty. Both Hellyer and Marchand admit that to accomplish any kind of solution, they are going to have to rely to a great extent on the commitment and full co-operation of the three levels of government—federal, provincial, and municipal. In the United States, however, it is this same reliance that has stalemated the Office of Economic Opportunity in its War on Poverty. This bureau was specially set up to slice through the tangles of government and get to the hard core of poverty, but the realities of politics have always dictated that spending money is simply a means to ensure the government continuing political control. The politician's political authority has never been challenged by the poor; the poor, as it has been proven, simply do not vote—they know that, for them, political promises are never kept.

And finally, there is simple bureaucratic intransigence; governments and their ministers come and go, but the civil service endures forever. It was bureaucratic intransigence that actually resulted in some F.R.E.D. and A.R.D.A. programs working at cross purposes, cancelling each other's attempts to combat poverty in Canada. For example, the federal decision to put money into the Maritime cities came only after five years of pouring it into rural areas—despite the fact that the regional governments argued all along that it should go to the cities and despite the economic reports with which they backed up their assertion.

Certainly politicians, social scientists, and organized labour are only too well aware of all the handicaps that threaten the success of attempts to deal with poverty through government channels. It is probably for this reason that the greatest interest is now concentrated on the guaranteed annual income as a possible solution to poverty.

At the February, 1969, educational conference staged by the Ontario Federation of Labour in Niagara Falls, there was a unanimous demand by all speakers for a guaranteed income. Reuben Baetz, executive director of the Canadian Welfare Council, John Eleen, research director of the O.F.L., Peter Brownstone, professor of the department of political economy at the University of Toronto, and Dr. Wilson Head, a member of the Metropolitan Social Planning Council, all called for the guaranteed annual wage in one form or another. It was Head who suggested that "an income of approximately $5,000 to $6,000 per year for a family of four, and $2,000 to $2,500 a year for an individual would be a good starting point."

The reaction from Ottawa was almost immediate. Finance Minister Edgar Benson appeared on CBC-TV News. He said that he had had someone in his department do some quick calculations. To provide tax exemptions to those earning $5,000 a year and less would result in the government's giving up 40 per cent of the revenue derived from personal income tax. (Total personal income tax revenue is about $2 billion.) To compensate for that, Benson said with a chuckle, everybody earning above $5,000 a year would have to pay twice the income tax they now pay. (For examples of unfairness in the tax structure, see Chapter 8, "Keeping the Rich That Way.")

Benson's calculations involved only tax relief for the poor and did not take into account the negative income tax, giving grants to the poor in order to provide them with a guaranteed annual income of $5,000 a year. In the United States, it has been estimated that by 1975 the lowest fifth of families on the income ladder will still have incomes of less than $3,000 a year. To lift them from poverty to an income level of about $6,000 a year would require $38.6 billion in 1975. A projected budget based on current needs (which includes the $1.5 billion now being spent annually on fighting poverty) anticipates a deficit for 1975 of $40 billion. It is hardly likely that the U.S. could then budget for an additional $38.6 billion expenditure. Obviously, a meaningful guaranteed annual income—either here or in the U.S.—is still a long way off.

Before he resigned his cabinet post, Paul Hellyer suggested that the poor be allowed to sit on civic committees and become involved in the decision-making processes that affect their lives. After all, who understands the problems of the poor better than the poor themselves?

During the United States' four-year War on Poverty, there was plenty of evidence of the poor's knowledge of what should be done. However, being poor does not necessarily condition one to accept middle-class values without question. The representatives of the poor sat on committees made up, for the most part, by people who believed that only middle-class guidance could remedy the problems of the poor. For example, in the run-down Cardozo area of Washington, the poor wanted day-care centres so that unemployed mothers could get out and find work. Middle-class social workers and government advisors blocked the centres because they feared such operations would emotionally damage the children. The result was a bitter clash of values and political fighting that blocked all progress.

In the fall of 1967, Ben Seligman, professor of economics and director of the labour relations and research centre at the University of Massachusetts, wrote a sad and depressing conclusion to his book, *The Permanent Poor,* which was published in 1968. It serves as a warning to the poor and a haunting reminder to those who are not:

> The War on Poverty is grinding to a halt. The expectations of many poor have been aroused. . . . But now, after several years of agitation, the Great Society seems to be no different from the Ordinary Society. The poor will return to their urban and rural slums, as quiescent as they have been through all the years back to the beginning of time. The promise has not been fulfilled, and it appears that poverty, even in an affluent society, has congealed and hardened into a kind of sub-culture that represents a social syndrome, an ineradicable condition.

Remember, there has already been one Canadian War on Poverty, but, as John Eleen of the o.f.l. points out, "It began and ended at the federal-provincial conference on Poverty and Opportunity in April, 1965."

✌2✌

Why did Charlie Wenjack Die?

The life expectancy of a Canadian Indian woman is twenty-five years; for a man, it is thirty-five. The infant mortality rate among Eskimos is 293 deaths per thousand, more than ten times the infant death rate for the population as a whole. The Economic Council of Canada has avoided making statements that racial discrimination is a cause of poverty, but there is no doubt that the poorest of the poor in this country are the Indians, the Eskimos, and the Metis.

There are now approximately 29,000 Eskimos, 60,000 Metis, and, by the 1965 census, 218,000 Indians. In that same year, the Indian Affairs branch made a survey which showed that 78.5 per cent of Indian households had incomes of less than $3,000 a year, 54.5 per cent less than $2,000, and 28.2 per cent less than $1,000. When Buffy Ste. Marie sings, "My country 'tis of thy people, you're dying," she is singing about right now.

It is possible that during his short and disturbed life someone may have taken a snapshot of Charlie Wenjack—one of those laughing, open-faced, blurred pictures one so often sees of children. But if one was taken, nobody knows where it is now.

There are five police pictures of Charlie, though. They are large, 8-by-10 prints, grey and underexposed, showing the thin, crumpled body of a twelve-year-old boy with a sharp-featured face. He is lying on his back, and his thin cotton clothing is obviously soaked. His feet, encased in ankle-high leather boots, are oddly turned inward. In one of the photographs, an Ontario Provincial Police sergeant is pointing down at Charlie's body where it lies beside the C.N.R. track. It is the exact spot where Charlie collapsed and died from exposure and starvation on a cold, wet night—just four-and-a-half feet from the trains that carry the white world by in warm and well-fed comfort. When they found Charlie, he didn't have any identification. All they got out of his pockets was a glass jar with a screw top. Inside were half a dozen wooden matches. They were all dry. And that's all he had.

Charlie Wenjack was an Ojibway attending Cecilia Jeffrey Indian Residential School in Kenora, Ontario. He became lonely and ran away. He died trying to walk 400 miles home to his father, who lives and works on an isolated reserve in northern Ontario. It is unlikely that Charlie ever understood why he had to go to school and why it had to be such a long way from home. It is doubtful that his father really understood either.

It's not so unusual that Indian children run away from the residential schools they are sent to. They do it all the time, and they lose their toes and their fingers to frost-bite. Sometimes they lose a leg or an arm trying to climb aboard freight trains. Occasionally, one of them dies. And perhaps because they are Indians, no one seems to care very much. So this is the story of how a little boy met a terrible and lonely death, of the handful of people who became involved, of a town that hardly noticed.

Even before Charlie ran away from the school, he was

already running hard just to keep pace with the bewildering white world he had suddenly been thrust into. He didn't start school until he was nine. The village he came from, Ogoki Post on the Martin Falls reservation, didn't have a day school. So Charlie was sent to the Cecilia Jeffrey School, which is run by the Presbyterian Church and paid for by the federal government. Some 150 Indian children live at the school but are integrated into the local school systems. Consequently, Cecilia Jeffrey is, for ten months in the year, nothing more than an enormous dormitory. And Charlie, who understood hardly any English, spent his third year in what is called a junior opportunity class. That means he was a slow learner and had to be given special instruction in English and arithmetic. In his fourth year, he wasn't quite good enough to go back into the grade system, so he was placed in what is called a senior opportunity class. But there was nothing stupid about Charlie. The principal during his last year, Velda MacMillan, believed she got to know him well. "The thing we remember most about him was his sense of humour. If the teacher in the class made a joke, a play on words, he was always the first to catch on."

Charlie wasn't a strong boy. In fact, he was thin and sickly. He carried an enormous, livid scar that ran in a loop from high on his right chest, down and up over his back. It meant that in early childhood his chest had been opened. Nobody knows exactly when or why. "Indian children's early medical records are practically impossible to track down," Kenora's public-health doctor, P. F. Playfair, later explained. The post-mortem that was later performed on Charlie by Dr. Peter Pan of Kenora showed that his lungs were seriously infected at the time of his death.

On a Sunday afternoon, when Charlie had only another week to live, he was playing on the Cecilia Jeffrey grounds with two friends, Ralph and Jackie MacDonald. Ralph, thirteen, was always running away—three times since the school term had started that fall. Jackie, only eleven, often played hooky. (In the three years he had been at the school, Charlie had never run away. But he had played hooky one afternoon just a week earlier, and for that he had been spanked by the principal, Colin Wasacase.)

The three made a spontaneous decision right there on the playground to run away. It was a sunny October afternoon, and they were wearing only light clothing. If they had planned it a little better, they could have taken along their parkas and overshoes. That might have saved Charlie's life.

Slipping away was simple. The school, a bleak institutional building, stands on a few acres on the north-east outskirts of Kenora. For the 150 boys and girls, there are only six supervisors. At that time, the staff were all new and still trying to match names to faces. (That same day, nine other children ran away. All were brought back within twenty-four hours.)

As soon as they were clear of the school, the three hit that strange running walk with which young Indian boys can cover ten miles in an hour. They circled the Kenora airfield and struck out north through the bush over a "secret trail" that children at the school like to use. The boys were heading for Redditt, a desolate railroad stop on the C.N.R. line, twenty miles north of Kenora and thirty miles east of the Manitoba border. Because Charlie wasn't as strong as the others, they had to wait often while he rested and regained his strength. It was on the last part of this walk, probably by the tracks, that Charlie picked up a C.N.R. schedule with a route map in it. In the following days of loneliness, that map was to become the focus of his longing to get back to his father. But in reality the map would never be more than a symbol, because Charlie didn't know enough English to read it.

It was late at night when the three boys got to Redditt; it had taken them more than eight hours. They went to the house of a white man the MacDonald brothers knew as "Mister Benson." Benson took the exhausted boys in, gave them something to eat, and let them sleep that night on the floor.

Early the next morning, the boys walked another half mile to the cabin of Charles Kelly. The MacDonald boys are orphans–their parents were killed in a train accident in 1965. Kelly is their uncle and favourite relative. Kelly is a small man in his fifties. When he talks, he has a nervous habit of raking his fingers through his grey, shoulder-length hair. Like most of the Indians in the area, he leads a hard life and is often desperately hungry. It's obvious he cares about his nephews. "I told the boys they would have to go back to school. They said if I sent them back they would run away again. I didn't know what to do. They won't stay at school. I couldn't let them run around in the bush. So I let them stay. It was a terrible mistake."

That same morning, Charlie's best friend, Eddie Cameron, showed up at the Kelly cabin. He, too, had run away from the school. Eddie is also one of Kelly's nephews. This gathering of relations subtly put Charlie Wenjack out in the cold. The Kellys had two teenage daughters to feed in addition to their nephews, and Kelly, who survives on a marginal income from welfare and trapping, probably began to wonder exactly what his responsibility to Charlie was. He said later that he and his wife, Clara, would refer to Charlie as "the stranger." The Kellys also had no idea where Charlie's reserve was or how to get there.

"He was always looking at this map," said Mrs. Kelly,

31

"and you couldn't get nothing out of him. I never seen a kid before who was so quiet like that."

Nobody told Charlie to go. Nobody told him to stay, either. But as the days passed, Charlie got the message. So, in what must have been a defiant attempt to assert his own frail existence, he would take out his map and show it to his friend Eddie Cameron, and together they would try to make sense out of it. And Charlie would tell Eddie that he was going to leave soon to go home to his father. But as Eddie remembers, Charlie only knew "his dad lived a long way away. And it was beside a lot of water."

On Thursday morning, Kelly decided he would take his three nephews by canoe up to his trapline at Mud Lake, three miles north of Redditt. "It was too dangerous for five in the canoe," said Kelly, "so I told the stranger he would have to stay behind."

Charlie silently played outside the cabin for a while by himself, then he came in and told Mrs. Kelly he was leaving; he asked for some matches. Nobody goes into the bush without matches. If the worst comes to the worst, you can always light a fire to keep warm. Mrs. Kelly gave his some wooden matches and put them in a little glass jar with a screw cap so they would keep dry. She also gave him a plateful of fried potatoes mixed with strips of bacon. Then he left. "I never seed him again," said Clara Kelly.

Nobody will know whether Charlie changed his mind about leaving or whether, out of loneliness and despair, he decided he wanted to see his friends one last time. Because instead of striking out east along the railroad tracks, he walked three miles north through the bush to Mud Lake. He must have really pushed himself, because he arrived at the cabin by the trapline before the surprised Kelly and his nephews got there in the canoe. All they had to eat that night was two potatoes. Kelly cooked them and divided them among the four boys. He didn't eat anything himself, but he drank some tea. In the morning, there was only more tea. Kelly told Charlie he would have to walk back to Redditt; there was no room in the canoe. Charlie replied that he was leaving to go home to his father. "I never said nothing to that," Kelly said later. "I showed him a good trail down to the railroad tracks. I told him to ask the sectionmen along the way for some food."

But Charlie didn't ask anyone for anything. And though he stayed alive for the next thirty-six hours, nobody saw him alive again.

When he left Kelly and his nephews and started out to walk home to his father, Charlie had more than half of northern Ontario to cross, over 400 miles. There are few areas in the country more foreboding. The bush spreads away from the railroad tracks like a bleak and desolate carpet. The wind whines through the jackpines and spruce, knocking down rotten branches in sudden crashes. The earth and rocks are cold brown and black. The crushed-rock ballast, so hard to walk on, is a pale yellow ribbon supporting the dark steel tracks. Close to the tracks, tall firs feather against the grey sky. And when a snow squall comes funnelling through a rock cut, it blots out everything in a blur of whiteness. The sudden drop in temperature can leave a man in a warm parka shaking with cold.

All Charlie had was a cotton windbreaker. And during the thirty-six hours that Charlie walked, there were frequent snow squalls and gusts of freezing rain. The temperature was between twenty and thirty degrees. It is not hard to imagine the hopelessness of his thoughts. He must have stumbled along the tracks at a painfully slow pace–in the end, he had covered only a little more than twelve miles. He probably spent hours huddled behind rocks to escape the wind, gazing at the railroad tracks. Somewhere along the track he lost his map or threw it away. Charlie must have fallen several times; bruises were later found on his shins, his forehead, and over his left eye. And then at some point on Saturday night, Charlie fell backward in a faint and never got up again. That's the position they found him in.

At 11:20 A.M. on Sunday, October 23, engineer Elwood McIvor was bringing a freight train west through the rock cut near Farlane, twelve-and-a-half miles east of Redditt. He saw Charlie's body lying beside the track. An hour later, a section crew and two police officers went out to bring Charlie's body back.

The section foreman, Ed Beaudry, was angry and bitter. "We tell this man he has to send his son to one of our schools, then we bring his boy back on a luggage car."

On the Sunday they went to pick up Charlie's body, intermittent snow and sleet blew through Kenora's streets. The church services were over, and the congregations from Knox United Church and the First Presbyterian Church, which face each other at Second Street and Fifth Avenue, were spilling out onto the sidewalks. Just two blocks west, at Second and Matheson, I walked into a hamburger joint called the Salisbury House. An Indian woman in an alcoholic stupor was on her hands and knees on the floor, trying to get out the door. None of the half-dozen whites sitting at the counter even looked at her. A young, well-dressed Indian girl came in and, with a mask-like face, walked around the woman on the floor. The girl bought a pack of cigarettes and then on the way out held the door open for the woman, who crawled out on her hands and knees and collapsed on the sidewalk.

One man at the counter turned and looked at the woman.

"That's what they do to themselves," he said in a tone of amused contempt.

The kid behind the counter suddenly turned, white-faced and angry. "No, *we* did," he said.

"We? No, it was the higher-ups, the government," replied the man.

"No," insisted the kid, "it was you, me, and everybody else. We made them that way."

The men at the counter looked at the kid with closed, sullen faces. Later, I tried to talk to him, but he wouldn't give me his name. "I just work here part-time," he said. "I work for the highways department. . . . I guess I'll have to learn to keep my mouth shut. Because nothing ever really changes around here."

Charlie Wenjack finally did go home—the Indian Affairs Department saw to that. They put him in a coffin and took him back to Redditt and put him on the train with his three little sisters, who were also at the Cecilia Jeffrey School. Colin Wasacase, the principal, went along with them too. Wasacase, in his early thirties, is a Cree from Broadview, Saskatchewan. He knows what Indian residential schools are all about. He has lived in them since he was a child and taught in them. He was at one such school at the age of six when he broke his left arm. The arm turned gangrenous and had to be amputated.

At Sioux Lookout, on the way home, the little party picked up Charlie's mother. She was taking tests for a suspected case of tuberculosis. From Nakina, they all flew 110 miles north to Ogoki. It's the only way to get to Charlie's home.

Charlie's father, grief-stricken, was bewildered and angry. In his fifties, he is known as a good man who doesn't drink and provides well for his family. He dug the grave and buried

Charlie, his only son, in the tiny cemetery on the north shore of the Albany River. He has decided not to send his daughters to school but to keep them at home. Wasacase understands that, too. His own parents kept him out of school for two years because another boy in the family had died in much the same way as Charlie.

There's not much else to say about Charlie Wenjack, except that on November 17 an inquest was held in the Kenora Magistrate's Court. Most of the people who have been mentioned in this story were there. The coroner, Dr. R. G. Davidson, a thin-lipped and testy man, mumbled his own evidence when he read the pathologist's report, then kept telling the boys who ran away with Charlie to speak up when answering the Crown Attorney's questions. When Eddie Cameron, Charlie's best friend, entered the witness box, Davidson unnerved Eddie with warnings about telling the truth and swearing on the Bible. "If you swear on that book to tell the truth, and you tell lies, you will be punished." Which seemed unnecessary because, as Crown Attorney E. C. Burton pointed out, a juvenile doesn't have to be sworn in at an inquest. Eddie later broke down on the stand and had to be excused. Davidson let Burton deal with the boys after that. Burton was gentle enough, but the boys were withdrawn and, for the most part, monosyllabic in their answers.

"Why did Charlie run away?"

Silence.

"Do you think it was because he wanted to see his parents?"

"Yeah."

"Do you like school?"

"No."

"Would you rather be in the bush?"

"Yeah."

"Do you like trapping?"

"Yeah."

Before the boys were questioned, the constable in charge of the investigation, Gerald Lucas, had given the jury a matter-of-fact account of finding Charlie's body. In telling it simply, he had underlined the stark grimness of Charlie's death. But it was now, through the stumbling testimony of the boys and in the bewildered silences behind those soft, one-word answers, that the full horror began to come out. No, they didn't understand why they had to be at the school. No, they didn't understand why they couldn't be with their relatives. Yes, they were lonesome. Would they run away again? Silence. And the jury was obviously moved. When Eddie Cameron began to cry on the stand, the jury foreman, J. R. Robinson, said later, "I wanted to go and put my arms around that little boy and hold him and tell him not to cry."

There were no Indians on the jury. There were two house-wives, a railroad worker, a service-station operator, and Robinson, who is a teacher at the Beaverbrae School in Kenora. In their own way, they tried to do their duty. After spending more than two hours deliberating, they produced a written verdict and recommendations that covered one long, closely written page of the official form. The jury found that "the Indian education system causes tremendous emotional and adjustment problems." They suggested that the school be adequately staffed, so that the children could develop personal relationships with their instructors, and that more effort be given to boarding children in private homes.

But the most poignant suggestion was the one that reflected their own bewilderment: "A study be made of the present Indian Affairs' education system and philosophy. Is it right?"

Charlie Wenjack died on the night of October 22, 1966. More than two years later, on Saturday, June 21, 1969, the Toronto *Star* carried a front-page report on the living conditions of Indians in and around Kenora. Written by staff reporter Glen Allen, it showed that almost nothing had changed. And the fact is that over the past four years there have probably been more marches, more protests, more investigating experts of all kinds, more over-all exposure by the mass media of conditions in Kenora than any other area in this country; yet, as the kid in the hamburger joint said, nothing really changes. I found some depressing echoes in Mr. Allen's report. He quoted a local lawyer, Jack Doner, who said that despite all the discussions and public alarms, the only solution really being considered "is a bigger and better jail." Mr. Doner said the same thing to me when I did the first story on Kenora for *Weekend Magazine* in July, 1965. It's obvious that provincial and local action hasn't gone very far, either in thought or deed. And the ancient punitive solutions are the only ones held on to. At Armstrong, Ontario, just 240 miles north-east of Kenora, the local school board will not allow Indian children to attend the local school, contending that the Indian parents are not taxpayers but squatters on crown land. So the children, like Charlie Wenjack, are separated from their parents for ten months in the year by being sent to residential schools hundreds of miles from their homes.

But the first part of 1969 gave no brighter promise than previous years to Indians across the country. Ottawa raised taxes and cut back public spending to curb inflation. Provincial and federal budgets were trimmed, and the first to feel the effects of all this were, of course, the poor, in this case the Indians. Around the Lesser Slave Lake area of Saskatchewan, some 3000 Indians and Metis continued to exist at a marginal level of subsistence—even as Premier Ross Thatcher promised yet another war on Indian poverty. And across the rural ghettos of northern Ontario, the Indian bands fed bitterly off their own despair, all the while listening to the Ottawa and Ontario governments wrangle about who had constitutional jurisdiction over their lives. Early in May, Chief Wilmer Nadjiwon, president of the Union of Ontario Indians, resigned from the Indian Advisory Council of the Ontario government's Indian Development Branch. He did so, he said, because he was "convinced that the government was not sincere" in its program to help Indians overcome poverty.

A few days later, the entire seven-man executive staff of the Ontario government's Indian Development Branch resigned, including the director, Joseph Dufour. Premier John Robarts' first reaction was that the men had resigned only because they had been looking for an excuse to do so. It was a weak defence, especially as it had been revealed earlier in the legislature's debate on spending estimates that the responsible minister, John Yaremko, had spent only $400,000 of the $1.4 million he had been given to spend for Indian development during the previous year. (See Chapter 7, "Keeping the Poor That Way.")

And across the country, the white man continued to bring his legal and political machinery into play whenever he wanted one more piece of land from the Indians in the name of progress, whenever he sought to impose his own kind of moral law on the native people. For example, in Manitoba, the former Conservative government of Walter Weir, despite the outcry of the public and of experts, proceeded with plans to allow Manitoba Hydro to divert the Churchill River in constructing a $1-billion power project that would result in high-level flooding of South Indian Lake. The flooding would wipe out two prosperous and self-supporting Indian and Metis communities of some 600 people who had never known the misery of having to depend on the white man's welfare handouts.

On June 20, 1969, a New Brunswick county court judge, in a bewildering display of judicial legerdemain, ruled that Indian rights granted in treaties dating from as early as 1725 were annulled by the Fisheries Act. The case went back to September, 1966, when Martin Francis, a sixty-six-year-old Micmac of the Big Cove Reserve, was convicted of fishing in Richibucto River with a net and without a licence, breaking a New Brunswick Fisheries regulation and the Fisheries Act of Canada. At his trial in January, 1968, before Judge Eric P. Richard, Francis maintained it was his right to fish in the Richibucto—free of any of the white man's laws. Furthermore, this right had been guaranteed by the white man himself in a treaty drawn with the Micmacs in 1725.

Judge Richard found Francis guilty, ruling that Parliament and the provincial legislatures were not bound by the terms of any treaty made before Confederation. Justice having been meted out, Judge Richard totally confused the Micmac by saying that he well understood why the Indians say "the white man speaks with forked tongue." The judge then proceeded to lash out against what he called "the ceaseless encroachment by the white man on the Indians' rights and privileges."

The farce didn't end there. Francis decided to appeal the conviction. The appeal was denied by Kent County Court Judge Claudius Leger, who actually read from the pertinent passage in the treaty "that the said Indians and their constituents shall remain in the districts before mentioned, quiet and free from any molestation of His Majesty's troops or his other good subjects in their hunting and fishing."

There was no doubt, said Leger, that the Indians of the Big Cove Reserve "were solemnly guaranteed by treaty or proclamation the right to hunt and to fish." However, he went on to say, under powers granted to the Government of Canada by Section 91 of the British North America Act, "Parliament has the right to enact legislation which infringes on the treaty rights granted to the Indians." In this case, the legislation was the fishing regulations. The most ironic fact about all these legal manoeuvres was that Francis had made his appeal with federal financial aid supplied by the Department of Indian Affairs.

But what was probably the most bizarre display of symbolic justice took place in April, 1969, at Pond Inlet in the Northwest Territories. Bizarre because of the pseudo-formal ceremony erected around the pathetic suffering of a young Eskimo girl, who unwittingly became the vehicle for the first criminal trial ever held in Pond Inlet and the investiture of Justice Minister John Turner as "the first Canadian to be admitted to the bar north of the Arctic Circle."

Pond Inlet is on the north shore of Baffin Island, 2,000 miles north of Ottawa and 430 miles north of the Arctic Circle. The accused was a seventeen-year-old Eskimo girl who came from a tiny Eskimo community near Pond Inlet. In August, 1968, she had given birth alone to a dead child. It is a criminal offence not to seek aid in giving birth to a child. In this case, it was obviously an unwanted pregnancy; the girl managed to conceal both the pregnancy and the birth from her parents. She hid the body of her baby in a box; two days later, she threw it from some nearby cliffs overlooking Eclipse Sound. Some passing hunters discovered the body a week later and handed it over to the R.C.M.P. detachment. A doctor on board the federal icebreaker *C.D. Howe,* which supplies settlements during the summer break-up, performed an autopsy; papers were passed back and forth in Ottawa, the R.C.M.P. were ordered to investigate, and the seventeen-year-old girl was charged.

Now, nine months later, the accused is standing in an elementary school classroom that has been turned into a makeshift court. Presiding is Mr. Justice W. G. Morrow, judge of the Northwest Territories, who has flown 600 miles from Frobisher Bay to hear the case. Also flown in for the case were the defence lawyer, David Searle, and the crown prosecutor, Orval Troy. In attendance is Justice Minister Turner and his entourage, who have joined the court's circuit of the eastern Arctic to witness justice being done. The accused has pleaded guilty. She doesn't speak any English, so proceedings are conducted through a local twenty-one-year-old Eskimo. Consequently, it is possible that much of the majesty of the occasion is lost upon the prisoner. At any rate, it is apparent later that she has understood little. Mr. Justice Morrow gives her a two-month suspended sentence under bond of $20, and she retires nervously to stand alone at the back of the classroom. Mr. Justice Morrow now presents Justice Minister Turner with a soapstone carving of the Canadian coat-of-arms and admits the minister to the bar. Turner pays tribute to the sacrifices made by Mr. Justice Morrow, Mr. Searle, Mr. Troy, and other territorial lawyers. "I think the people of Canada," says Mr. Turner, "can be assured their law does travel to the Pole."

About this time, someone discovers the criminal still standing around at the back of the classroom, uncertain of whether more is wanted of her. So the interpreter gently leads her from the room, telling her, yes, she can go now. A little later, the white men climb into their planes and fly away.

Over the past ten years, Indians in this country have been trying to escape from the ghettos that many of their reserves have become–according to the E.C.C., only one-third of the 2,200 reserves in Canada have the economic potential of supporting their present population–but they have found only ready-made ghettos in the cities.

Winnipeg is now silently and desperately struggling with the problems that an influx of 20,000 Indians and Metis has brought to the city. With few skills and fewer resources to deal with white society, they have become trapped in the bureaucracy of welfare and the tenements of slum landlords, who operate on what is known as Cockroach Capitalism. One Winnipeg alderman privately admits that if the city were to enforce its health and housing by-laws properly, thousands of Metis and Indians would be thrown out on the street.

The late Winnipeg Magistrate Isaac Rice saw the same people as the source of much of the petty crime he had to deal with in his court. And in February, 1969, on the C.B.C. television program *The Public Eye*, he bluntly suggested that sterilization was the logical social solution. Later on in the program, a group of Winnipeg aldermen matter-of-factly discussed the advantages of a sterilization program. Magistrate Rice and the aldermen were ordinary people, and they used ordinary words to express themselves. But behind that commonness was the horrifying reality that they were seriously considering the use of such a repressive solution against a class of people who, at the bottom of the ladder, were already defenceless. And whose advantage would such a sterilization program serve? Certainly not the Indians'! The only conclusion to be drawn is that it is really the affluent in our society who want to be protected from the demands of, and relieved of their responsibility to, the people who originally owned this country.

It was against this backdrop of despair and bitterness that

43

Jean Chretien, Minister of Indian Affairs and Northern Development, unfolded another sweeping new policy for Indians at the end of June, 1969. Briefly, the new plan would end the federal trusteeship of Indian lands. The reserves would be returned to the bands to be disposed of as they saw fit. All Indian and federal government agreements would be annulled, the Indian Act repealed, and the Department of Indian Affairs phased out of existence. The Indians would then become the responsibility of the provincial governments.

The new policy was supposedly built upon recommendations that had come out of many lengthy consultations Chretien and federal officials had held with Indian leaders during the previous year. But the reaction of those Indian leaders was swift and bitter. Chief Wilmer Nadjiwon of the Ontario Union of Indians labelled Chretien's policy "cultural genocide." Chief Harold Sault of the Union of Northwestern Ontario Native Organizations said, "The white man has done what he has always done; he has listened but he has not heard us." And in Alberta, Harold Cardinal, president of the Indian Association of Alberta, threatened civil servants with violence if they came to the reserves to discuss implementation of the new policy before the Indians were ready to. "Our advice to bands in this province," said Mr. Cardinal, "is to physically escort federal commissioners off the reserves, and, if necessary, forcibly evict them." In its own way, the statement was an accurate appraisal of how much the Indian people trusted the federal government in 1969.

Down and Out

DOWN AND OUT IN TORONTO

In Toronto's Allan Gardens, old men are lying on crumpled newspapers spread out on the dry summer grass, their frail and spindly arms folded under their chests like the wings of fallen angels. Their 1948-styled Sally-Ann suit coats are folded neatly by their heads, along with their hurt and battered boots.

Scotty lies so that only his head is shielded by the circumference of shade beneath a young maple tree. He has taken off his torn and grubby white shirt and is lying in a green, silken singlet that is trimmed with yellow piping around the neck and armholes. The material is soiled but seems strangely rich against the sickly greyness of his skin. On the back of the green singlet is the crest of a girls' private school. And on the hem, which hangs outside Scotty's pants, a white tag carries the red-embroidered name, "Elizabeth Fryers." I squat near his head, and he turns to eye me with that blind, defensive hatred and anger that he always seems to carry in his face. It's a bad face. The eyes are too close together; a cluster of warts running along his right eyelid make it droop malevolently. The murky pupils swim in yellow whites that are threaded with red veins. He has severe rhinitis; it keeps his nose running and encrusted with mucus. The flesh of his nostrils is swollen with bad booze and burst blood vessels.

He once told me he was forty-two. It's possible. He could also be sixty.

Scotty doesn't want to talk to me today—he thinks I am a usurper. A few nights ago, he showed me that you could wash your feet in the hand-basins at the bus station at Bay and Dundas between 12:30 and 1 A.M. At that time there is no attendant on duty to bawl you out. I was there last night, washing my feet and my socks, when suddenly there was Scotty at my elbow, hissing, his ugly face full of venom, "What the hell are you doing in my sink, you son-of-a-bitch?"

But now, when I push half a bottle of Parkdale wine across the grass toward him, his face is weak with eagerness. Without a word, he drinks carefully and quickly at the corner of his mouth. The bottle is inside one of those brown paper bags with string handles. The words "Toronto Public Library'" are stamped in big letters across one creased and grubby side. I found it this morning in a litter basket outside city hall in Nathan Phillips Square. "That's a lotta good reading you got there, a lotta good reading," and Scotty giggles at his own joke. He can't really let go of the bottle and makes only a tentative gesture to push the paper bag back across the scrubby grass.

"Keep it. I've had enough." It's true. The cheap wine has cracked my head open under the hot afternoon sun. I take off my boots and lie back under the shade. Scotty doesn't say anything until he finishes off the wine. For a moment there is some colour back in his face. He doesn't offer thanks, but he is grateful.

"Hey kid, did I ever tell you about the lady doctor who

examined me at the General?" He giggles madly to himself again. It is his current sex fantasy. I've heard it many times, and I don't really want to hear it again. It is just too obvious, Scotty. What human being would even want to touch you, let alone have you embrace him? It would have to be Christ himself. The rejection is in my silence, which is how everything is really said down here on what the middle class calls Skid Row. What does Skid Row mean, anyway? It's just that the middle-class mind has a label for just about everything it doesn't have any contact with. A few weeks ago, on c.b.c. Radio, I heard a well-known Toronto newspaperman describe Scotty and the other people I have been living with these days as "human sludge." Well, for that part of the world that counts humans as a form of currency, I suppose it's a clever enough label.

I wonder what labels that guy would have come up with last night, if he had been with me as I sat at the kitchen table in a two-room apartment over a Queen Street store. It was a dingy, low-ceilinged little place with newspapers pinned over the windows. The noise and the fumes from the traffic grinding by outside filled the room. Across the table from me sat an old man in his seventies. He held his three-year-old granddaughter on his lap, and a boy of about five roamed the room. The kids drank Coke and munched chips from a plastic bag. The children badly needed to be cleaned up. The boy kept asking for his brother, but the welfare people had taken the elder children away. At irregular intervals, their mother, who is not even thirty, would come into the apartment with a man and take him into the other room. Half an hour later, they would leave. Each time it happened, the boy stood quietly behind his grandfather's chair. Some self-defence mechanism in him did not want to witness the strange comings and goings of his mother. She was turning $10 tricks to raise bail for his father in jail on an assault charge.

The old man is going blind, and perhaps last night he was grateful for that; although he seemed to pay no attention to what was going on, there is no doubt that he was ashamed and embarrassed at what was happening to his family. We talked across the table. He is a good old man to talk to. He spent most of his life toiling in a Nova Scotia coal mine, but he could never free himself or his children from poverty. And now, in the helpless bitterness of old age, he is forced to watch his family turning into petty criminals. He kept telling me about his youngest son, now in prison. "He's not a gunman," he often repeated, meaning that he was not a hood, not a seasoned criminal. The old man is living on the old-age pension of $109 per month, and he lives in a $15-a-week rooming house where he can't even cook on a hot plate. He gets by on a dollar a day for food.

That's where I first met him, in the rooming house, shuffling down the hall to the lavatory, an old shirt flapping around his skinny haunches. He was very upset because he had just moved from another rooming house, and, through some bureaucratic mix-up, he was no longer getting his pension cheque. The landlord could have arranged an interim payment of some kind with one of the city welfare agencies, but he didn't want to be bothered. It wasn't until I promised to pay the old man's rent for that week that he let the old guy stay. Later, the old man invited me to go with him to visit his grandchildren. And that's how I came to be there that night. His daughter-in-law stopped once to offer me some pills—they looked like amphetamines—but for the rest of the time she ignored us, locked away, tight and silent, in her own feverish despair.

Besides the kitchen table and the four wooden chairs, the

only furniture in the room was a white plastic radio. The old man and I listened to it during the lulls in our conversation. In a few days, the United States was planning to put a man on the moon, and this small, white, plastic voice told us that the famous L.E.M. alone had cost $100 million to develop and almost as much again to test. The old man couldn't get over it. "A hundred million bucks just to see if it works," he kept muttering. Then, later, when I was helping him wash the kids in the sink, he looked up and said, "You know, I can't even get another twenty-five dollars a month for disability. They say I'm not blind enough yet."

And now, the next day, as I lie here in Allan Gardens, I look up at the small maple giving me shade. Fifty, sixty years from now, when it's a full-grown tree, I wonder if there'll still be men like Scotty lying under it. And in the meantime, how many stars will men have journeyed to? And in this country, I wonder, will there still be slums where children watch their mothers turn tricks to get their fathers out of jail?

Scotty is asking me for some money. I don't have any. We are joined by another bum whom everyone calls The Frog. It's easy to see why. He has a great, lipless mouth that circles around the lower part of his chin like a great razor slash. His chin drops imperceptibly into his neck and short, squat body. He doesn't have any money either. Without ever really deciding anything, the three of us start ambling in the direction of Union Station. It's a good place to bum for small change. People are getting out of cabs, buying tickets and magazines. They have money in their hands. And when you have a dollar's worth of change right there in your palm, it's that much harder to turn down a bum asking for a dime or a quarter. Scotty claims that he once found a wallet there with twelve dollars in it.

49

We go by way of Bay Street, which is usually busy and, as everyone knows, has plenty of resources. The Frog and Scotty work both sides of the street; they bum with a smoothness and circumspection that, unless you are accosted by them or watch them closely, leaves most passers-by unaware of what is going on. The Frog does it by sliding into people. He puts one foot almost between their legs. As they turn to one side to get around him, he croaks out his request. "Gotta dime for a man in trouble?" His great lipless mouth doesn't even move. When people give, they usually do it in the same movement that takes them around and away from him, assisting him in his surreptitious manner. And The Frog always keeps going. He never looks back, not even to say thank you. I follow at a distance, doing what the bums call "phoning mother long distance." I walk behind them, checking all the pay phones on the street and in the entrances of restaurants, pushing the coin-return button and searching the slot for nickels and dimes someone might have left there after attempting a call that didn't go through.

When I get to the intersection of Bay and King, a uniformed cop is walking over to an old man who is tunelessly blowing a mouth organ and holding out one cupped hand. The Frog has disappeared, and Scotty is waiting for me across the street. We walk west along the south side of King. Over our heads towers the great, shining, black box of the Toronto Dominion Centre. As we pass the entrance to the underground shopping mall, I suggest to Scotty that we go down; there is air conditioning in there, and we can cool off. He has never been inside and is reluctant to go, feeling safer on the hot, grimy sidewalks. But he is hot. He looks sick and drawn out. His face is blotched and pulpy—his must be a dreadful body to drag around. So we go down and sit on a wide, uncomfortable, backless bench. Three smartly dressed matrons, already sitting there, immediately leave. Scotty sits there, hunched and anxious, gazing into the open doors of an expensive-looking dress boutique. Inside, all kinds of young women in mini-skirts are wandering around the dress racks. They take down wildly colourful garments, hold them against their bodies, and, abruptly swinging thighs from hips, strike poses in front of a mirror. There is something strangely mechanical about it all, as if they are silently moving through a well-rehearsed routine. Even their arm movements are like those of puppets.

We really are in another world. Well-dressed men and women walk by us. Their eyes hit us and quickly slide away. Scotty wants to leave. To help him relax, I roll him a cigarette. He could make one himself, but I don't want his fingers, which he uses to wipe his running nose all the time, grubbing around in my tobacco. I ask Scotty what he thinks of the women. He gives a grunt of disgust. "You gotta pay for it," he says, "you know what you're getting then."

A long time ago, when Scotty was eighteen and a telegrapher for c.p.r. in some godforsaken northern town, he brought his childhood sweetheart out from Glasgow and married her. Then one night he came home early from his night shift and found her in bed with one of the yard foreman. He beat them both almost to death, or so he says, then divorced her.

"Paid for it after that," he always says. "Know what you're getting then." It's strange to sit here, look at him, and realize that once he was young, moved by love and violent passion.

But now we've suddenly got trouble on our hands. A swarthy, middle-aged man with a potbelly, dressed in a janitor's uniform, carrying a broom and a long-handled dustpan, shows up beside us. He also has a cop in tow. The cop is young, with a very white face and a long, sharp nose. He is bored with what he sees. He just came down here to cool off, too. But the guy with the broom is mad. "These bums spitting on the floor," he says in bad English.

Scotty is full of contempt. "Ahh, go sweep up your poodle shit," he snarls at the janitor.

"Okay, boys," says the cop, "let's move along." But he doesn't have his heart in it. He has his eyes on the long-legged girls moving around down here.

"What for?" I ask. "We're just sitting here having a smoke. It's a public place, isn't it?" I turn to the janitor. "Anyway, show us where we are spitting." For some stupid reason, everybody looks down at our feet. While we are all looking down, a saleswoman from the dress store appears before the cop.

"Officer," she says, pointing at Scotty, "this dirty old man has been sitting here exposing himself."

There's a ten-second silence while the cop struggles with this one. It sort of knocks me back, too. Maybe Scotty was, he's a sneaky old guy. But I'm certain that he was too uncomfortable to pull anything like that down here. And he once told me that he only does it to get arrested in the winter, when he needs a warm cell. Besides, I think it's pretty funny coming from this woman. She's dressed in a mauve miniskirt that ends at her crotch. Above, she has a see-through blouse with no brassiere, just a few strategically-placed mauve polka dots. She even has mauve eye shadow.

"Just a minute. I've been sitting here all the time and I know he wasn't. I'll say it in court. And that's where you'll have to make it stick," I say, pointing to the Mauve Peril. The cop is staring at her polka dots instead of worrying about all the paper work he has suddenly gotten himself into.

Right away she starts backing down. "I don't want to get involved," she says, working on the cop, massaging his eyeballs. "I just want you to get them out of here, away from the front of my store."

The cop can't tear his eyes off her blouse. Over-confident, I push it too far. "Maybe," I suggest, "you're the one who should be arrested."

Her eyes are blank, but the cop understands. Bums aren't supposed to talk like that. The white face swivels around. "You," he says, "shut up!" He's got a soft, mean voice. He leans into me, his long nose wrinkling like a rabbit's, trying to smell my breath but not wanting to take down a lungful. "You stink," he says, "and it's not booze." Some day, somebody is going to break that long, white nose for him. He is trying to figure me out, too young and lippy for a bum. He's looking for a pigeonhole. *The bum's got to be a pervert.* You can see his face tighten up as he makes his decision. He apparently decides I'm one of those young homosexuals who, for whatever reasons, sometimes team up with older bums.

"You," he says, making the pronoun sound like filth, "or whatever your kind call themselves, are going out that way, and your old girl-friend here is going out the other way, and don't let me ever catch you back here again." And he gives Scotty a sly prod in the kidneys to get him going.

Outside, I wonder if I should go around the block and find Scotty, but I conclude that I've brought him enough trouble for one day. I decide the cop is right about one thing though; I do stink. So I make my way to the Stephanie Street Public Baths, which offers the best deal in town for fifteen cents—a hot shower with soap and towel supplied.

LIVING WITH AUTOMATION IN WINNIPEG

Hear it! The crunching smash of twenty-four bottles of beer, all splintering against each other as I misdeal on the packing machine. Smell the stink of the warm beer pouring over my clothes, washing over the sour sweat of my body. I can feel the unheard curse as I toss the wet, mangled carton down the rollers for some poor bastard to sort out. And back to the mother-eating machine where the bottles are already starting to pile up on the conveyor belt. The ten-second delay bell starts ringing. The jangling vibrations echo in my skull, and the foreman comes running over, screaming incoherently. How the hell can I hear him over the roar of four acres of machinery and the teeth-jarring rattle of 25,000 bottles, all clinking against each other as they ride down the hundred yards of clanking metal conveyor belts.

But don't try to figure out what the foreman's yelling, you'll only lose more time. The bottles will back up all the way to the pasteurizer, the thirty-second delay hooter will start whooping like an air-raid siren, then they'll pull you off this job for sure and send you down to the washers, so forget him and just keep moving. With your left hand crush the right hand corner of the next empty carton and ram it on the hydraulic lift. Kick your heel down on the pedal to send the drawer up. The bottles drop through the metal leaves this time with a nice *thonk*, thank God! And even as they are hitting the bottom of the box, stab the pedal with your toe to bring the drawer back down. Before it stops, spin off the loaded carton with your right hand to send it in the direction of the sealing machine. Don't wait for it to clear the drawer, reach for the next empty carton with your left hand. But you have to waste time, reaching in to push the "filler" down flat. And without even looking at him, you scream at the filler-man, "Look what you're doing, you son-of-a-bitch! Can't you even put these lousy pieces of cardboard in straight?" He, seeing only your lips curling, snarls obscenely back. Never mind him either. He's been here fourteen years, paying his union dues, kissing the foreman's ass. Look at the zombie, pot-bellied on all the free beer, draggy-eyed from a lifetime of night shifts, skin like a corpse, embrace your fellow industrial worker!

A group of tourists are coming through the brewery. Cowed by the noise, they shy away from the machines, cringing behind the protective eyeglasses issued at the front office. They stop to wonder at the frantic activity around the packing machine. And we, the sweat running down our faces, our shirts soaked, our hands and feet doing five different things at once, turn smiling and scream the crudest of obscenities at the women. And they, unhearing, smile and mouth thank you, then walk on with another uncertain smile for the monkeys in the freak show.

All this ten hours a day. Surrounded by four or five other workers who endlessly fold cardboard cartons in a bored blur of hand movements. Their hands turn flat shapes into square boxes, insert handles and fillers that will keep the bottles separated from each other. Behind them on scores of wooden platforms await thousands of unfolded cardboard cartons. They are literally unfolding a forest of trees between their hands. Other men tend the monotonous machines. One feeds thousands of bright little labels into slots; each label costs one cent, but that's more than the beer inside the bottle is worth. "Everything else is taxes and profit," that's what the brewmaster said. Another man sits dreamily beside a lighted yellow panel. In hypnotic progression, each bottle passes briefly in front of this panel before being filled with beer. The man tries to catch the ones that are still jammed with trapped mice, cigarette butts, and old safes, even after going through the washers.

All the men are wearing the same dingy uniforms, green workpants and shirts. They are my brotherhood, and we are men of our time, working in feverish, mute activity, unable to communicate, drowned out by the roar of our age, the ass-end of this industrial epoch. Run this packing machine, you slob. Pack twenty-four bottles of beer every six seconds. Ten cases every minute, six hundred in an hour, six thousand in a ten-hour shift. Fill all those empty bottles full of beer so all the leisure-programmed people in this country can drink their beer in creepy bars and dirty, men-only beer parlours. Pack so the whores on Main Street can tease their fancy men over a couple, so the businessmen can pull on a three-o'clock beer and ease a contented fart. And you, you sad bastard, work! Work to fill up those empty boxes with bottles of beer so that all those beautiful people out there can piss it away.

Don't waste time thinking about the absurdity of this effort. Just pack and think about the $125 a week you're clearing. Pack and forget about the bills you can't pay. Pack and don't look at the man going around giving out pink slips. Just keep packing, you dummy. Because while you're sitting there running that machine, with the sweat running down into your eyes, with your hands and feet going like an epileptic's, they're already building a machine to do your job. And brother, nobody can hear a word you're screaming.

LIFE ON THE POGEY

It was twenty-two degrees below zero yesterday. And I stood with the rest of the unemployed against the frigid limestone walls of this city. We watched the warm, sleek automobiles, halted steaming at the intersections. From inside, peering through mist-wiped frost shields, I could see the warm and well-stuffed. They gazed curiously at the frozen, lean-ribbed men who, with wordless bitterness, understand who really own this country.

Earlier I went to ask for my pogey, to collect my unemployment insurance. Shuffling forward to the "Claims Taking" counter, I tried to smile, to be pleasantly articulate, but I only ended up mumbling and pushing forward the forms and the small, round-cornered pink card that announces to the Unemployment Insurance Commission, and to everyone else, what I am, where I am, and what I want to be. The swarthy, pimple-faced girl behind the counter wiped up what is officially me with one hand and, without even glancing at my face, rapped out from between her discoloured teeth, "Take-a-seat-at-the-left-sir."

Faceless, I sat down with the rest of the faceless, perched on rows and rows of folding wooden chairs. From there we watched a parade of the unemployed. Most were serious, others giggled self-consciously, and a few were pathetic, even ludicrous. But as each one surrendered his little pink card, he too became faceless. The girl behind the counter was totally without curiosity about the people who came to her.

Her impersonality only heightened my feeling of impotence and inability to deal with the bureaucratic process. I wondered. How will they know what to do with me? How could anyone make a decision about me with just that much written on a few pieces of paper? But slowly, the people I sat with became little pink cards again. The shambling and bulbous civil servants tacked toward us across the tiled floor. For some reason, they didn't come around to face the chairs but from the side squeaked or hoarsely bellowed into our ears the names of this city: "Alex Prokopchuk, Jesus Marinez, Edwin Ronald Shaw, . . . Schrieber . . . Ustawszawski . . . Gambetti." One by one, after a brief count of comprehension, they lurched to their feet and staggered past our peripheral vision, leaving the rest of us to sit stiffly facing the front. A broken-faced, broken-assed hooker came in with her pimp, and he was the only one who didn't have a card. He sat down with her, whispered in her ear, then sidled away. She shyly looked around. No high rollers in this crowd. Then, like the rest of us, she silently faced front.

I became a face again when a middle-aged redhead with a crumbling, heavily-powdered face murmured my name and beckoned. I shuffled along at the pace she set across the floor to a little cubicle.

"What company did you work for last?" she asked. "And how long?" I explained. No reaction—she just made a note. "Can I get any money today?" I asked, feeling embarrassed, as if I were begging money from a stranger.

"No, you have to wait two weeks," she replied, still writing. "Go to this office," and she wrote down an address. "Your call time is 11:00 A.M., January 23. Don't be late."

I thanked her. For what? But she was already stern up, wallowing across the Claims Taking floor, whispering for another face.

January 23, 11:00 A.M. The big hall is unbelievably overheated, almost steamy. The sickening smell that comes from too many people standing around in heavy clothing forces its way through my nostrils and into the back of my throat. But then the senses adjust, and the smell recedes. I find my line and get into it.

The man behind me, a grey, dull face, is droning on to nobody in particular, saying the things that everyone hears in this building during the winter. "Just like the Dirty Thirties . . . gets worse every week . . . shouldn't let those goddam D.P.'s in . . . taking the jobs from Canadians . . . what we need is another war . . . this is what it's always like before another war."

I can't think of anything to say that will help him, so I turn around and face the front, trying to estimate how much money I will receive, from $17.50 to $30 a week. How can you even start to live on that? And then there's a $2,000 debt. But don't start thinking like that or you'll wind up like the guy behind you. Concentrate on the immediate problem of getting this money today so that at least you can go out and buy some groceries.

It's a slow line, and it's half an hour before I get to the counter. A thin-necked kid with glasses takes my callbook, murmuring, "First call, eh?" He pulls out a card-index drawer, riffles through it fast. Too goddam fast. Nothing. He double-checks, again nothing. He's a cheery kid. "Nothing here for you today. Take your callbook over to the special interview counter and wait in the line under A to D."

Unnerved, I fumble with my callbook, peer stupidly around until I find my line. I stand behind a narrow grey carcoat. A hand extends from the left sleeve, working a steel tape measure like a yo-yo. Nobody talks in this line, and there's not much of interest to look at. In a glass-panelled office to one side, a great spraddle-legged machine clacks away with a mechanical rhythm, ejecting from its bowels neatly stacked index cards. A good-looking blonde with heavy legs is wearing a crazy, purple, fuzz-leafed helmet, which, except for the odd red woolen cap, is the only violent color in this place. After a while, I realize everyone is intently watching what happens to the people at the head of the line, watching to see if they go to the cashier's cage or straight out the door. After keeping count for twenty minutes, I estimate that fewer than one in five is getting a payment cheque. And for the first time my confidence that I'm going to get this money crumbles. My stomach turns and writhes, leaving me as naked and desperate as any man in this room. How the Christ am I going to eat this week?

After about forty minutes, my turn finally comes. Across the counter is a haggard-faced woman of about thirty-five.

She wears glasses with rhinestones across the top of the frame. It leaves her with a permanently quizzical look. Mrs. Bad News. She silently takes my callbook. Again there's a drawer of index cards. Again nothing. Again the double-check. Again, again nothing.

"Sign this card please, and if your cheque comes through before next week it will be mailed to you. Otherwise, report same time, same place next week." And she's already reaching for the next guy's book.

There's nothing to do but walk with eyes downcast along the line to the glass doors, past the loafers in the lobby, and into the bleak winter street.

On the way home, I pawn my wristwatch for $4 to buy groceries. When I get home, I find my wife in the kitchen, pale and angry, holding the baby in her arms. The bailiff is in the living-room. He has piled our miserable sticks of furniture in a heap in the middle of the room. He tells me that if I pay the two months back-rent I can have my furniture back. I reply that I have no money because I have no work. But if he gives me a couple of days, I'll try to borrow some money. No, he can't wait, he has to have it today.

He is a fat, tall man, no older than me. I have to hold my body stiff to try and stop the anger shaking through me. And I try to hold on to my voice so that it doesn't run away from me. I ask him how he lives with himself, earning a living in such a crummy way. "I don't like it," he says, "but I can't find work in my own line. In this job I'm paid by commission. I have a wife and kid, too. I have to put bread on the table."

I tell him that I'd sooner starve than make money this way. There is a red flush under his flabby cheeks, and I can see that he really is ashamed. But he takes the furniture anyway and locks us out of the apartment.

4

The Hidden City

Imagine a city, a walled city of 350,000 adults and more than 1.1 million children. A city larger than Winnipeg, as big as Vancouver, but different. The weird thing about this city is that it is without men; there are only women. If you can see such a city in your mind's eye, then you are looking at the real and enormous number of abandoned and forgotten people who live silently among us. Because, you see there are that many women in this country, bringing up their children on marginal incomes and the subsistence that is welfare. Officially, there are only 55,000 women on Mother's Allowance, but there are thousands of others living on various forms of welfare payments because the bureaucracies of welfare departments say they do not qualify for Mother's Allowances.

The women are single heads of families. Chained to an extremely low standard of living, they struggle bleakly to survive and keep their children with them. Most of the time they fail. Not because they don't have the will, but because the law, the impersonal and illogical bureaucracy of the welfare system, and the mindless disregard of society stack the odds too high for any human being.

But before going on to document the plight of this enormous number of women and children without men who form a large portion of the total number of poor in this country, let us take a moment to examine the outlines of female poverty–women with men and women without. Because the truth is that the poor in Canada are not only the Metis, the Indians, and the blacks, but women–and in the most overwhelming numbers.

If you add the number of women who are on welfare, the number of working women who are heads of families and survive on less than $3,000 a year–the figure sociologists have arrived at to mark the dividing line between poverty and affluence–and also add the single women who work for less than $3,000 a year and the elderly poor women, then you have a group five times the size of all the poverty-stricken racial groups put together. The majority of the poor in this country are women; it is as simple as that. By conservative addition, there are some 3 million of them in Canada, almost one-half the number of women over sixteen.

But you don't have to believe me. As far back as 1964 the Ontario Federation of Labour produced a report which revealed that more than 6.5 million people lived on or below the borderline of poverty, that 2 million were in the richest province of all, Ontario.

There is a summary to the c.f.l. report which is really a list of the strikes against an individual ever climbing up from poverty into the affluent classes. Right at the top of that list are the assertions that, a) you're not going to make it if your family is on welfare, and b) you're not going to make it if you belong to a family whose head is female.

The terrible thing about these figures is that they are growing rapidly. Today there are 350,000 women who are single heads of families, but only ten years ago there were less than 200,000 women in the same position, and the country's welfare bill was one-third of what it is today. Ontario alone spent $227 million on welfare in 1969.

But more importantly, the forces that create such huge masses of poverty-stricken individuals—those forces which have created an even greater gap between the poor and the affluent in the last decade of the technological era—have not even been recognized, let alone confronted, by the government agencies charged with this responsibility. To live on welfare today is to live like a character out of Dickens. In St. John, New Brunswick, there is a deserted mother who has five children between the ages of five and fourteen. The Social Assistance Department allows her $16 a week for food and household expenses. A survey in the area by the Nutritional Division of the Department of Health and Welfare showed that the woman would have to spend a minimum of $28 a week for food alone. In other words, if the woman spent all her money from Social Assistance on food, she would still be purchasing only a little more than half of the minimum her five children need. And, of course, if the woman worked in an attempt to make up that extra amount, her earnings would automatically be deducted from her Social Assistance.

But this attitude of repressive deprivation toward women is not only held by those municipal and provincial officials who dole out welfare; it is also deeply imbued in the thousands of employers who pay salaries of less than $3,000 a year to 50 per cent of the female labour force. And remember that every third worker is a woman (there are some 2.4 million of them) and that women constitute more than 40 per cent of the labour force in the white-collar and service industries.

When I pointed this out to a Toronto social worker, he replied, "The $3,000-a-year figure doesn't mean anything because it includes all the married women who are working part-time." The figure does include married women who work part-time, but they constitute only about 15 per cent of all women workers. And the social worker was not informed enough to know that his criticism was meaningless in the scale of poverty, because the fact is that 70 per cent of the married women in the labour force work either full-time or part-time because their husbands make less than $3,000 a year.

Even more shocking is the fact that only 10 per cent of working women make more than $5,000 a year; at the other end of the scale, a third of all single working women make $1,700 or less. And if the white woman is poor, the Indian woman is even worse off. As a group, their earnings are almost non-existent.

For women, wages have nothing to do with competence. Toronto workers probably enjoy the highest wage levels in the country, yet an energetic young lawyer I know, who makes a minimum personal income of $25,000 a year, recently phoned to ask if I knew of any intelligent young woman who might like to go to work in his law office. I replied that I knew two but didn't think he would be able to woo them away from their present jobs for less than $125 a week. "Are you kidding?" he asked, "for $400 a month I can get a trained and experienced legal secretary. For $70 a week I can get someone who I can teach how to run the show." Then, laughing at my naïvete, he hung up, all the while exclaiming to himself, "A hundred and twenty-five a week!"

The lawyer's attitude is reflected in the figures that are put out by the Dominion Bureau of Statistics on the wages of Canadian women. Despite all the provincial statutes requiring equal pay for equal work, employers use a rough rule of thumb: always pay a woman half of what a man in the same job is worth. In a recent study by Jenny Podoluk of the D.B.S. (included in the *Profile of Poverty in Canada* by the

Special Planning Secretariat), she showed that men between the ages of thirty-five and forty-four with only elementary school education earn an average yearly wage of $3,312. A woman in the same age and education bracket makes $1,560. The situation does not improve as you move up the scale of education; in fact, it becomes comparatively worse. Men with four or five years of secondary school and between the ages of twenty-five and thirty-four earn $4,536 yearly; the women in that bracket make $2,595. A male university graduate between thirty-five and forty-four makes an average of $7,928; a woman of similar qualifications receives $4,343. Which means that a woman with a university degree usually makes less than a man with only four or five years of secondary school education, and she will probably never match the earnings of a man who has not been to university. The most ironic note in this area is that female university teachers, doing the same job as men and holding the same degrees, are paid an average of $1,200 a year less.

What happens to women who try to stand up for their rights and demand equal pay? Take, for example, Lois Beckett, who was a policewoman for more than fifteen years in the Sault Ste. Marie area. In December, 1967, having been denied membership in the all-male Police Association, she sued the Sault Ste. Marie Police Commission for the same pay as that of a police constable. She got as far as the Ontario Supreme Court, where Mr. Justice R. I. Ferguson brusquely rejected her claim. In his judgement, he said, "It is contrary to all the world's economies that a woman should receive equal pay to that of a married man." He went on to say that Miss Beckett's actions were undermining the morale of the force and "a menace to its *esprit de corps*." Miss Beckett appealed and gained a retroactive pay raise to second-class constable. (First-class status is usually acquired after two years' experience.) Since then, however, her duties have been confined to those of a clerk-typist—and she has been denied admission to the all-male Police Association.

But such a reaction from our judiciary shouldn't be so surprising. After all, it's no secret that the legal profession still looks askance at women lawyers. Judy La Marsh admitted in January of 1969 that her admittance to a prestigious law firm was blocked because a senior partner didn't believe women should be lawyers—even if they had been cabinet ministers.

But let's examine the kind of world the prejudiced masculine mind has created and perpetuated for women who are poor. In their world, welfare is a bureaucratic nightmare. In its 1964 report, the Ontario Federation of Labour accurately described welfare as "a hodgepodge of public and private arrangements with administration at various levels of government. Other than political considerations, no overall standards are observed and administration at the local level is generally inefficient."

Official recognition of this chaotic structure was given January 15, 1969, when Health and Welfare Minister John Munro admitted it was time that the provinces and the federal department got together to work out a better system. They were brave words, but the truth is that although the government is paying out something like $50 million a month for welfare in this country, it really has no idea to whom the money is being paid or how it is being paid out.

Through a complicated series of cost-sharing agreements, Ottawa pays roughly half of the welfare bill, but the provinces jealously guard the authority to administer welfare budgets. Thus the mechanics of how the money actually trickles down into the hands of mothers on welfare are left to the administrators of every city, town, and municipal government. Each, of course, has its own method of payment. Some give cash, others cheques, and some pay in vouchers and chits which are honoured only at local stores. And, of course, each politician has his own idea of how much the poor need to get by. Ultimately, the confused multiplicity of bureaucratic systems keeps the poor on a treadmill of marginal living while simultaneously robbing them of pride and the ability to get back into society. I sat once and listened for three hours as a Manitoba village reeve and his four councillors debated how much coal a deserted mother and her three children needed to get through the winter. All the while, the woman was present.

Minor bureaucrats also use welfare payments in any number of ways to remind the poor of their dependence. In the summer of 1968, Mrs. Albert Cloutier of Kempville, near Ottawa, spent eleven days going two or three times a day to the post office to see if the monthly $279 welfare cheque—paid to her husband for a disability—had arrived. It was their sole income, and they have six children between the ages of four and sixteen. "I was in a panic," she said. "We had nothing to eat." She was finally told that the town clerk had the cheque. Apparently, the municipal authorities wanted some car wrecks removed from the Cloutier property—and apparently no one had bothered to find out that Mrs. Cloutier had had the cars taken away two weeks previously.

The situation is not much better in the big cities. Michel Blondin, an official in the Montreal Council of Social Agencies, says, "In big cities, welfare agencies are looked on like any other institution such as the Post Office. A person who needs help cannot express his point of view. The agency in turn has policies, and even if it wants to listen, cannot."

And it is in the large cities that women on welfare gather. Their thinking is that only in the city will they perhaps be able to find a job and some measure of independence. But

67

decent housing is impossible to find in the cities today without paying exorbitant rents, and, even though Welfare Departments allow a maximum for rents, it is never enough, and families have to deduct from their food money to make up the difference.

In a brief to the Hellyer Task Force on Housing, a group from a Toronto low-income housing development reviewed a family's welfare budget. Instead of taking out the rent money first, they deducted essential amounts for food, clothing, medicine. All figures were based on government-set minimums—there was, of course, no money left over to pay the rent.

It is in the decaying pockets of downtown slums that fatherless families find themselves caught in the vicious circle of poverty and welfare from which there is no exit, and which, as this example from the St. Christopher House in downtown Toronto shows, inevitably destroys the family.

Mrs. C. is the widowed mother of twin girls. Physically disabled, she receives a pension of $65 a month. Being physically limited, she has had difficulty controlling her twins, who are now temporary wards of the Children's Aid Society. The family lived in a wooden house up a back lane that Mrs. C. had purchased with part of her small income; last year, the house was condemned as a "typhoid trap." A mortgage provided money for plumbing repairs, but it is obvious that Mrs. C.'s limited income cannot pay for maintenance of the building. At present, the bathroom is unheated and not insulated. The roof leaks. Some electrical outlets require fixing. Painting and repairs are needed inside and out. The court has ruled that Mrs. C. must sell or rent this house and move to a new environment before the family can be reunited. She has three months before the case is reviewed. Obviously, Mrs. C. cannot solve her problems before the case is reviewed. It is just as obvious that she cannot really solve anything on $65 a month.

Out on the open prairies, women in poverty battle against an even more harsh and bitter isolation. In Manitoba, for example, there are 2,800 women living on welfare who are the sole heads of their families. However, there is another group of mothers, about 900, who cannot qualify for the Mother's Allowance because they have not been separated from their husbands for the required minimum period of twelve months.

And when a woman does manage to stand on her own feet, there are always the idiosyncrasies of bureaucracy to remind her of her inequality: for example, the Manitoba Hospitalization and Medical Schemes insist on treating a married couple as a unit, whether they are living together or not. One woman, who is the sole support of her family after being separated from her husband, had her wages garnisheed to pay a family hospitalization bill that she wasn't even aware was outstanding. After the bill was paid, she asked that she be registered as an individual so that she wouldn't be faced with the embarassment of another garnishee. She was told she could only do so with her husband's consent. He refused, so the woman is still registered on a family plan and, of course, has to pay for it.

Examples of how women in poverty suffer the petty harassments of the law are not confined to any one province. In a northern British Columbia town, a woman struggled to keep her six children with her after her husband committed suicide. She sang and played the guitar in bars to make money. When the Welfare Department objected to her children being left alone every evening in charge of the eldest girl, who was only fourteen, she waded through all the red tape that one has to go through to become enrolled in an adult re-training course. Her two eldest children were placed in temporary foster homes. Somehow, she managed to take the others with her. In the middle of her retraining course in Vancouver, a bailiff appeared with a warrant for her arrest. It was for non-payment of taxes on the small house she owned in her home town.

In January, a young Toronto woman who was separated from her husband went to a discount store to buy some clothes for her children. Her husband had assured her that he had already deposited her monthly maintenance cheque. He hadn't, so the cheque she gave for the clothes bounced. She was charged with false pretence. The case was finally dismissed, but, for the miserable amount of $9.60, the woman was dragged into court, had her name reported in the newspapers, and lost a much-needed day's pay.

The economic position of women and children who are on their own is best articulated in the Report of the Manitoba Volunteer Committee on the Status of Women.

The biggest single and continuing problem of the sole-support mothers is a basic financial insecurity and a subsistence level of living which they have no real hope of improving. When there are court awards payable by husbands, they are unenforceable if the husband chooses to avoid payment. The mothers live in constant fear that the payment will be late or will not be made at all. When they receive state assistance because they cannot manage by themselves, it is given at a very low level and if they can find extra work they do not improve their own economic circumstances because the basic aid is then decreased. Also, if they receive maintenance awards and then try to improve their circumstances over and above the low basic award given, they are likely to find their maintenance award also cut back due to their "improved economic circumstances".

But what happens to the children? For the son or daughter of poverty, youth and early adulthood are only bleak extensions of a deprived childhood.

Any possibility that they may escape through their own youthful vigour and enterprise is quickly and brutally killed.

Numerous surveys and reports across the country have shown that children from poor homes are the first to drop out of school. In groups where the family head makes less than $4,000 a year, only one in eight children continues past the high school level. A Royal Bank of Canada study shows that only two per cent of those with only an elementary school education ever make it into the $10,000-a-year bracket. Canada Manpower figures show that 20 per cent of those who don't finish grade school are unemployed; seven per cent of those who finish grade school but not high school are unemployed, and only three per cent of those with at least a high school diploma remain unemployed. The statistics also reveal that more than a third of the unemployed are between the ages of sixteen and twenty-four.

Surely these figures are the best argument that current welfare and education policies do not work. In the end, they only perpetuate and multiply both the problems and the numbers of the poor.

For the older woman who has spent the greater part of her life bringing up her children on a marginal income or welfare, middle-age brings no escape. Studies show that most continue to live on welfare because the only alternative is a menial, low-paying job. A fortunate few manage to find some self-respect and independence holding down a clerical job at the minimum wage. Almost a quarter of all women over forty-five are widows, as are half of all women over sixty-four. At that age, a woman can expect to live another fifteen years. For widows, this means being deprived of their husband's old-age pension, moving to a small room, living on less.

The problems of these women and children will never be solved by money distributed according to budgetary policies that depend on the whims of various political parties.

It has been calculated that in the five years since the United States embarked on a vast effort to deal with poverty through government channels—to the tune of a billion-and-a-half dollars a year—that, at best, the government programs reached no more than six per cent of the poor. The government agency that was supposed to streamline and co-ordinate all the programs, the Office of Economic Opportunity, strangled in hopeless political deadlocks with all the levels of federal, state, and local government.

There has also been a pathetic impotence in the attempts, no matter how well-intentioned, of the middle class to understand the poor. For example, read this classic excerpt of jargon from a sociologist's report on a downtown Toronto slum:

The lower-class subculture of the urban jungle is distinguished by the female-based family and the marginal male. The male, whether husband or lover, is physically present only part of the time, and is recognized neither as a stable nor dominant member of the household. He participates only minimally in the exchange of affection and emotional support, and has little to do with the rearing of children. The woman tries to develop a stable routine in the midst of poverty and deprivation; the action-seeking man upsets it.

If you have lived in the slums, as I did, you know all that jargon really means is that for a woman with three kids on welfare, a man is only a sometime thing. And you really don't have to be told why—at least, not by a sociologist.

But hopefully, for the first time, the women who bear the

real burden of poverty in this country are being listened to. And it all happened quite accidentally. When all those nice middle-class ladies with their associations and service clubs pressured the government into the appointment of a Royal Commission on the Status of Women, they never thought for a moment that everywhere they went they would be hit in the teeth with the simple fact: the real problem of women in this country is that they are poor. The ladies were even less prepared for the tirades that came from women like Doris Wilson of Regina and Kay Dixon of Victoria, who blasted the nice service club women for treating the poor as a "project" and asked why one of their own wasn't sitting on the Commission. Chairman Anne Francis had to admit that poverty was one aspect of the status of women that "all the women's groups who pushed for a Commission hadn't spent much time thinking about."

Surprisingly, the poor women also know very well what's good for them. They want proper day-care centres for their children so they can get out and earn a living. Instead of a fluctuating subsistence level of welfare, they want a guaranteed minimum income. It would help them rent decent housing and would also free them from the petty harassments of bureaucracy. They want enforcement of equal pay statutes. They want better protection under the law and from the law. They want better retraining programs so they can break out of menial jobs they are caught in. But most of all, they want special and urgent help for their kids. The mothers know that they probably won't find a way out of the poverty trap in their own lifetimes, but they desperately want to find an escape hatch for their children.

It is possible that this enormous number of Canadian women has at last established a beach-head on the consciousness of society. But they've still got a long way to go. They've got to overcome the apathy and ignorance of their own sisters, women like the secretary of a politician I went to interview. "But don't you think," she said, "it's really their own fault that they lose their husbands and become poor?"

They're also going to have to organize and become more militant. As Stan Little, president of the Canadian Union of Public Employees, points out: "Only one-sixth of Canada's 2.4 million working women are organized. And although twenty-five labour organizations in Canada have a majority of female members, there has never been more than one woman to serve on the thirty-member executive council of the Canadian Labour Congress." The ladies who don't have unions to infiltrate, the ones sitting home eking out an existence for themselves and their children on welfare, are going to have to study the example set by the women of Harlem. There, when they want a day-care nursery and can't get one, a few hundred of them get together on a certain day and take all their children to the local welfare office. Then they go out to work. After a few hours of coping with a thousand children, the welfare officials are ready to give the mothers almost anything.

In the end, those 300,000 Canadian women are going to have to smash their way out of the walled city of poverty. The affluent are never going to open the doors for them.

❦5❦

The Forgotten Miners
of Newfoundland

*"...that's the way we Newfoundlanders are.
We don't take anything from any man that
we don't pay for in blood and sweat."*

The snow swirls out of the white void that is the Newfoundland sky, and Jack Fitzpatrick gazes out of his kitchen window, not really seeing the snow. For once his eyes are calm, perhaps because he is unwinding a movie reel of images out of his memory. He is talking about the day he first went to work in the fluorspar mines of St. Lawrence, at the age of seventeen. Then he mentions the name of a miner, Isaac Loder, who is being buried today, and Fitzpatrick is suddenly again in the present. Abruptly, he stops talking. He turns his face away from the window, and for a moment that pale face swings, and his eyes dart nervously around the kitchen. Nobody speaks. The only sound comes from a steaming kettle, gently hissing on the stove.

Jack Fitzpatrick is forty-four, and he is waiting to die. He has already been waiting for four months, and he has only a few more months to live.

His eyes have come to rest on his hands. Wordlessly, he spreads them over the design of red roses on the transparent plastic tablecloth. They are still a miner's hands. The fingers are large and square-ended. The tendons are thick and rope-like as he agitatedly tears an empty cigarette package into tiny strips.

But there are only the hands left. Fitzpatrick was never a big man, but his frame is already gaunt. He has lost about thirty pounds. The flesh has left his face, making his eyes seem abnormally large. The skin is stretched tight across his skull, revealing the temporal artery, a swollen, pulsing cord across the top of his bald head. His skin, incredibly white and feverishly luminous, acts as a veil for the disease that is eating away inside him. Every few minutes Fitzpatrick takes from his trouser pocket a soiled handkerchief and wipes the sputum from his mouth. Then he returns to his brooding, his shoulders hunched up in his blue workshirt, his fingers tearing the strips of cardboard into even smaller pieces.

It is very quiet in the kitchen. His wife, Harriet, a heavy woman, sits with her hands on her knees, looking down at the worn red and white squares of the linoleum. She has four sons living at home, still going to school. She is no doubt preparing herself for widowhood. She will have plenty of company; in this tiny community of just over 2,000 people, there are sixty-nine widows. And in the wooden frame houses that are scattered around the small natural harbour of St. Lawrence, there is not one family that has not lost a father, a brother, or an uncle to the mysterious, malignant disease that comes from working in the fluorspar mines. And fluorspar mining is the sole industry in St. Lawrence.

In the past twenty years, more than a hundred men have died; almost a whole generation of miners has been wiped out. And of the few men left in the community who are between forty-five and fifty-five years of age, seventeen are grievously ill. Fitzpatrick is only one of them.

"How do you pass the time?" I ask him.

In this oppressively silent kitchen, my words and my question sound absurd. All around me are signs of a life that has struggled against but never quite freed itself from poverty. And there has been nothing in Fitzpatrick's life to prepare him for this period of waiting and inactivity. And what does time mean to a man who is waiting to die? But he answers me politely, in the soft, pleasing accents of the Burin Peninsula.

"Well, I'll tell you, b'ye. When I'm all right enough, I goes down the hill for a ways. Coming back I take a couple of spells . . . to rest, y'know."

Another long silence. Harriet takes the kettle off, sits down.

"Do you know what it is you've got?"

"The doctor tells me I've a bit of the dust," he answers, using the miner's term for silicosis. "And I've got something a little better than that . . . a little better than that," he adds with a murmur. Without looking up, his wife says gently and matter-of-factly, "He's got what they all had. What they all died from. It's the same what killed his friend who they're burying today."

They're burying today. On my way to see Fitzpatrick in the morning, I unexpectedly encounter the funeral cortegé of his friend. The procession winds its way down the gentle slope of Water Street, past the miners' ugly, square houses, painted in violent yellows and greens. On the left is the harbour, the water a sullen, cold grey. Behind the houses are the desolate, snow-strewn hills, barren and stark. Here and there, silhouetted against the winter sky, are the lonely spectres of the deserted head frames, still standing over abandoned mine shafts. And over it all a cold wind is blowing snow flurries almost parallel to the ground. At the head of the procession, a young miner carries a large unpainted wooden cross. Attached to it are black and white streamers that flutter in the wind. His fingers are cold, and he shifts his grip on the cross. Behind him comes a battered green pickup truck. In the back lies the simple wooden coffin of Isaac Loder. Standing around the coffin, holding onto the sides of the pickup for balance, are the pallbearers. They are also miners, and the strips of white cloth bound to their right arms contrast with their dark winter clothes. Behind the truck come the mourners.

They are taking Isaac Loder to the graveyard that lies by the dirt road leading out of this little Newfoundland mining town. They are taking him to join his brothers. There was Peter, who died on September 9, 1963. He was forty-one. And Verno, who died April 13, 1962. He was forty. Isaac was forty-eight. Isaac was a powerful man of two hundred pounds who, unaided, could lift a loaded, one-ton ore cart back onto the tracks. But the pallbearers won't have much difficulty today; when Isaac died two days ago, he weighed seventy pounds. Isaac died of that terrible wasting disease, cancer of the lung, as did his brothers. A fourth brother, Dave, is in poor health now. "I guess my number could be up next," he says. (He died two years later, in April, 1969.)

And those are the men of the Loder family. They were all miners.

It is the same disease that is inexorably killing Jack Fitzpatrick as he sits at his kitchen table gazing out the window. I have seen his medical file. There is an X-ray that shows a massive, darkening growth around the base of the hilum of his left lung. The shadows are the cancerous cells, feeding off the living tissue. A letter in his file, signed by the radiolo-

78

gist, concludes that although there is no valid diagnosis, in all probability Fitzpatrick has lung cancer.

When he says no valid diagnosis, the radiologist means that no doctor has been able to cut Fitzpatrick open to make absolutely sure that he has cancer. But in the last few years, very few of the miners who have died in St. Lawrence have submitted to surgery. There's a good reason for it. They have seen too many of their fellows go to St. John's to have a lung removed, only to return home to their families and die horrible, painful deaths. By the time the lung is removed, the cancer has already entered the upper bronchial tubes. The severed bronchia becomes infected, finally ruptures, and the infection pours into the pleural cavity left by the removed lung. The pleura becomes filled with pus, literally gallons of it, which has to be removed through an incision in the chest wall. It is a painful way to die. Fitzpatrick knows that. He saw his own uncle die that way.

"I told them," he says, "they can take all the tests they like, but they're not going to get me on the table."

When Fitzpatrick becomes too weak to be cared for at home, he will be moved to the small, six-bed male ward of the St. Lawrence Memorial Hospital. That's where Edward Clarke was when I met him. He had cancer of the lung. A few weeks later he died. I also met Randall Turpin there. They hadn't found cancer in Turpin yet, but the doctors in St. John's removed the lobe of his left lung in 1954, and, ever since, Turpin had been classed as a pulmonary cripple. Beset by lung infections, pleurisy, pneumonia, bronchitis, he was unable to work. Turpin, his wife, and their four children somehow managed to get by on the $166 a month he received from Workmen's Compensation.

I asked him if he would ever let any of his sons go to work in the mines. "No, sir," he replied in a quiet, emphatic voice.

"I'd put a bullet in him first. Better to do that than have him end up like me." (Turpin died two months later, in June, 1967.)

If death is that which gives definition to life, then life for the past forty years in the town of St. Lawrence has been defined in the bleakest of terms. At 7 P.M. on November 18, 1929, a tidal wave smashed against the rocky head of Blue Beach Point, surged through the narrow entrance to the harbour, and destroyed the small commercial fishing fleet that had kept St. Lawrence a self-supporting community.

In 1932, when a New Yorker named Walter Seibert arrived on the Burin Peninsula, the people were living on welfare handouts—$1.80 a month for each person. Children suffered from rickets; scurvy and pulmonary tuberculosis were common.

Seibert told the villagers that they were living beside one of the richest deposits of fluorspar in the world, that fluorspar was an essential ingredient in steel- and aluminium-smelting operations—why, if everyone turned to, in a couple of years St. Lawrence would have a booming industry. In March, 1933, a freighter arrived with a hold full of second-hand mining equipment. The men of St. Lawrence unloaded it without pay. The St. Lawrence Corporation was formed, with Siebert retaining full ownership and control, but the people of St. Lawrence were encouraged to think of it as "their mine." They believed in it. They worked for fifteen cents an hour. They waited months at a time for their pay-cheques. When they arrived, they were only bits of paper, because there was no money in the bank to cover the cheques. The local merchants took the cheques and carried the St. Lawrence Corporation until there was money in the bank. If the cheque was for five dollars, and a miner's wife bought four dollars' worth of goods, the merchant tore off a piece of brown wrapping paper and wrote her an i.o.u. for one dollar. For years, those little pieces of brown paper were better currency than the cheques of the St. Lawrence Corporation.

The first ore was taken from crude opencast pits, but these filled too quickly with water. In 1937, the first shaft was sunk, and then began the terrible underground agony of the men of St. Lawrence. Men who, for generations, had earned their living on the open sea.

Of the men who sank the first shaft at the Black Duck Mine, there are only a handful left. One of them lives two doors from Jack Fitzpatrick. His name is Rennie Slaney, and although Slaney doesn't get out much now, he's still a very tough old guy.

"How are you?" I ask him.

"Ahh . . . staying ahead of the undertaker, b'ye," he replies with a harsh, high-pitched laugh.

Slaney is a bandy-legged little man. Before he became disabled, he worked underground for more than nineteen years, first as a mucker, then as a shift boss, until he worked his way up to mine captain. And that was in the days when the miners worked under the most primitive conditions imaginable. He can tell you stories about working hundreds of feet underground in drifts so plugged with dust and smoke you couldn't see the man working beside you—you could only hear him. It was a time when the mine owners used cost-cutting techniques that have long since been outlawed. Ventilation was nonexistent. Dry drills threw dust and dirt back into a miner's face from a distance of two feet. In the hoist shack, the operator kept a tally chalked on the wall of the number of ore buckets each shift took out of the mine. "If it was fifty," says Slaney, "then your shift tried to make it fifty-two. There was no bonus. Every man wanted to show he was as good as the next. And that's the way we Newfoundlanders are. We don't take anything from any man that we don't pay for in blood and sweat."

They paid. Slaney can tell you what it was like to come off an eight-hour shift and lie on the ground coughing your guts out until you vomited blood for twenty minutes at a time. And you believe it, because when you stand beside Slaney you can hear his bronchial tubes wheezing and straining for air. And you can hear the junk bubbling in his lungs as they strain and bang away, trying to get the air out again. Slaney suffers from chronic bronchitis, obstructive emphysema, infective asthma, and a condition called corpulmonale, which means that he is prone to heart attacks because the alveoli – the tissues that perform the chemical exchange of gases in the lung – are hardened in such a way that Slaney can get the air in but has difficulty getting it out again.

Although Slaney's condition is directly a result of the conditions he worked under for more than nineteen years in the mines owned by the St. Lawrence Corporation, he doesn't get Workmen's Compensation. The Newfoundland Workmen's Compensation Act covers only miners who have silicosis or cancer of the lung. Slaney is still fighting to get some compensation, in the same way he has fought over the past fifteen years to get it for some twenty other miners from St. Lawrence – by badgering the Workmen's Compensation Board in St. John's.

But Slaney is much more than a fighting survivor. He is the chronicler of St. Lawrence's dead and dying. In a simple, black-covered scribbler, he has lists of names that cover three pages.

The first page is headed: *Deceased – Underground Workers*. Here are the names of Newfoundland families who have lived on the Burin Peninsula for more than 200 years, and beside each name there is the letter L, which means the man died of a disease of the lung, or there is a short notation:

Joseph Squires L
Howard Pike L
Gregory Turpin (cancer of the spine)
Onslo Mullins L
Celestine Tarrant L
Arcule Slaney, Senior L

There are ninety-three men on the list. The youngest was thirty-two, the eldest sixty. There is another list of thirteen men who were surface workers and who died in the same way. Then there's a final list of twenty-eight men who are alive but so ill they cannot work.

According to Slaney, only thirty-five men and their families have received compensation. He first began making his lists in the late 1940's. "That's when we first started dying," he says. Miners would be sent to St. John's to be treated and cured of tuberculosis–which they had–but they would come home and die. "And," says Slaney, "nobody could explain to us what the men were dying from." Among them was his own brother. Slaney started to write letters to doctors in the provincial health department and to members of the Workmen's Compensation Board, but nobody seemed to pay much attention.

People seemed to dismiss Slaney as a complainer, a troublemaker. Then, in 1960, Dr. A. J. de Villiers and Dr. J. P. Windish of the federal Department of Health discovered that the miners in St. Lawrence were exposed to high doses of radiation from radon gas present in the mine. Suddenly, Rennie Slaney, with his letters and lists of names, made sense, for now there's no doubt in anyone's mind that the radiation in the fluorspar mines of St. Lawrence has a lot to do with the various forms of cancer that are killing the miners.

Dr. de Villiers stayed on to examine miners and compile data. In 1964, he published two papers in the British *Journal of Industrial Medicine* that showed the incidence of lung cancer to be twenty-five times higher in St. Lawrence than in the province as a whole.

In a preface to his second paper, de Villiers wrote, "It appears that the main factor causing the high incidence of carcinoma among the miners was the high level of radioactivity in the air and water in the mines." Yet–incredibly–nobody bothered to inform the miners what was going on. Slaney accidentally came across a copy of de Villiers' reports in September, 1965. He passed them on to Aloysius Turpin, then president of the St. Lawrence Workers' Protective Union.

By the time that the radioactive atmosphere of the mines was discovered in 1960, the Aluminum Company of Canada subsidiary, Newfoundland Fluorspar, was the only mining company left operating in the area. The St. Lawrence Corporation, owned by Walter Seibert, had terminated its mining operations on the Burin Peninsula in 1958, and Alcan purchased the St. Lawrence Corporation's properties. It also hired many of the miners who had been working for years under the abysmal conditions of the Seibert mines. In doing so, Alcan inherited the responsibilities of its former competitor.

Since it began mining operations in 1940, Alcan had conformed to all the regulations of the Department of Mines, and its reaction to the discovery of the mines' radioactivity was the installation of additional ventilating equipment. The theory was that the new machinery would exhaust the radon from the mine and bring the radioactivity down to a somewhat arbitrary level set by the federal Department of Health for workers exposed to radiation hazards. The truth is that nobody really has very much information about the effects of radioactivity on health. When radon is inhaled, it is thought to deposit extremely fine radioactive particles in the lungs. These particles are suspected of causing lung cancer.

With the figures that are now available, in de Villiers' studies, it seems that any miner who worked from thirteen to fifteen years underground before 1960, when the new ventilation equipment was installed, stands a very great risk of contracting lung cancer.

No medical authority will guarantee that there is no longer a radiation hazard in the Newfoundland fluorspar mines. Dr. de Villiers won't, and Dr. Brian Hollywood, who runs the St. Lawrence Memorial Hospital, says, "Only in ten or twelve years will we be able to say definitely yes or no." Hollywood works for the provincial health department, and no physician has been more personally involved than he in the tragedy of the St. Lawrence miners. It has been his duty to tell miners when they could no longer work, and he has attended them as they awaited their slow, inexorable deaths.

"They are a unique and courageous people," he says. "I have never heard a miner complain. I have to ask them, 'Where do you feel pain?' and only then will they tell me. And to the end they do their best to remain cheerful." Hollywood has probably been the most outspoken critic of the lack of interest in the miners' families shown by the government and the mining company. He describes the financial compensation that has been paid families as "a mere pittance." In 1967, a widow received $75 a month and $25 for each child under sixteen. The average number of children in a St. Lawrence family is five.

Between 1960 and 1967, twenty-nine miners died of lung cancer; twelve others died from other diseases that can be directly attributed to working in the mines. Meanwhile, Slaney stepped up his badgering of the Workmen's Compensation Board. He complained that nothing was being done for those miners who were ill or dying of diseases that were not considered compensative by the w.c.b. He pointed out that a widow couldn't live on the present compensation payments. And how, he asked, could a widow with three children find work in St. Lawrence, where, aside from a few small stores, the sole employer was the mine?

Finally, in January, 1965, the Newfoundland government issued an order-in-council to form a committee that would review the Workmen's Compensation Act. Someone asked Slaney to prepare a brief. Slaney sat down at the battered old typewriter on which he had already written so many letters to the w.c.b., and, in three terse pages, he told the committee exactly what the people of St. Lawrence had suffered since the first mine shaft was sunk. But it wasn't until February, 1967, that Slaney's brief was tabled in the Newfoundland legislature. It was included in the committee's report. The immediate effect was dramatic. The St. John's *Telegram* thought so much of it that the editor headlined the story "A National Disaster," and ran Slaney's entire brief. Premier Joey Smallwood immediately put the issue on ice by calling for a Royal Commission to investigate conditions in St. Lawrence. On a cbc-tv show, he admitted that he personally would never go down in any mine; the "real problem in St. Lawrence," he decided, "is mainly psychological."

The miners in St. Lawrence were not impressed by the Royal Commission. The chairman was Fintan J. Aylward, a lawyer and former president of Smallwood's Young Liberals. The members were Dr. Bliss Murphy, a radiologist for the provincial Department of Health, Frederick Grover, Deputy Minister of Mines, and Dr. W. D. Parsons, a consultant for the Workmen's Compensation Board who worked with de Villiers in 1960.

The miners would have been more optimistic about the Commission's objectivity if its members had been recruited from outside the ranks of Liberal government supporters and the provincial bureaucracy, which had never exhibited a sense of urgency about their plight.

In the town of St. Lawrence, the mine's image is not exactly a shining one. Mayor Fabian Aylward says, "There's a debt owed to these people, and somebody should pay it. You would think that after all the thousands and thousands of dollars' worth of ore the mine has taken out of this town, they could put some money back into it, but they haven't put a nickel back."

In 1967, the mine was paying an annual grant of $10,000 to the St. Lawrence Council in lieu of taxes. It also donates $1,000 a year to each of the two schools. There are about 240 men on the mine's annual million-dollar payroll.

Every year Alcan takes ore worth $2.25 million from the mine and ships it to Arvida, Quebec, for smelting.

Other than acknowledging that the cancer-stricken miners have died courageously, Alcan has not exhibited much interest in offering extra financial aid to the dying miners or their families.

"Certainly Alcan has the resources to move in," says I. S. Decarie, Alcan's co-ordinator of public relations, "but then what would be the commitment to our other 20,000 employees and their dependents? Such a move could have repercussions throughout the whole industry."

"Perhaps," said Dr. Frank Brent, Alcan's medical director, "as Canadians, we should each of us reach into our pockets to see how we could help the people of St. Lawrence." A remarkable statement from a man who works for a company that clears $80 million yearly profit after taxes.

In the last few months of his life, Jack Fitzpatrick continued to pay, out of his compensation money, $5.40 a month to the life-insurance plan which was coupled to his pension fund. He could draw on his pension only if he lived to be sixty-five. When he died, his wife and four sons, ranging in age from nine to eighteen, received $20,000.

After working twenty-seven years underground, Fitzpatrick was making $2.16 an hour. Until he worked his final shift on October 10, 1966, and Dr. Brian Hollywood told him he was through at the mine, he had never been sick in his life before, never missed a shift. He would go months without a day off, because he could work as a pump mechanic and get in extra shifts on Saturdays and Sundays cleaning out the sumps in the mine. But he didn't even get an aluminum watch, because you have to be with the Aluminum Company of Canada twenty-five years, and Jack Fitzpatrick didn't last that long.

Between the spring of 1967, and July 8, 1969, ten more miners reported to Dr. Brian Hollywood with what Jack Fitzpatrick had described "as something a little bit better than a touch of the dust." Four of those men have followed Fitzpatrick to the crowded graveyard on the hill that overlooks the bleak little mining town. "Living conditions haven't changed very much," says Dr. Hollywood. "It's still very hard on the widows and children." It is true that welfare payments have been raised from $75 a month for a widow to $100, and the $25 subsidy for each child has risen to $35 a month—but total payments to any one family must not exceed $300 a month. The average St. Lawrence family has five children.

On July 20, 1969, the report by the Royal Commission had yet to be released, but Rennie Slaney would never see it —he died that day, still trying to get his Workmen's Compensation. His widow is living on a handout of $30 a month. Obviously, officialdom thinks that Slaney didn't leave enough of his blood and sweat in the fluorspar mines of St. Lawrence. But then, that is how the Newfoundland government has always punished the working man who tried to stand up for his rights.

∿6∿

Images of Poverty in Saskatchewan

Saskatchewan, spaced-out space upon space. The colours are all raw, yellow, brown, and green. Saskatchewan in the droughts of late autumn, dry fields of stubble, the earth shorn of its wheat. Dust hangs in the white, exhausted air, moving like sandpaper down your throat. It plumes pale and heavy behind the pickup trucks as they bank over the gravel roads. The dust always rising, clouding the baleful yellow sky, filtering the sun to an angry red. In the haze, the wings of a red-tailed hawk turn to blood as it dips and soars over the rambling little village of Batoche, last stand of Louis Riel and his general, Gabriel Dumont. Also the last stand of the poor and dispossessed of this country. But now, on this hill, there is only an untidy little graveyard with its forsaken Metis names. To one side there is a peeling marker with a plaintive message, "Remember Our Heritage." In the centre stands a drooping wooden Indian cross. Below, the South Saskatchewan River sweeps past in a graceful, mindless curve.

Saskatchewan under the sudden thunderheads that fill the enormous empty sky. The lightning is terrifying. It whips across the prairie, ripping open the canopy of rain. Walking along the highway, there is no shelter in all this space, only the ditch by the road, where you lie with the rain smashing heavy and cold like a blow against your back. It is the heavy rain that doesn't stop, and work-worn men weep with rage in the fields, and in their madness run crouching, trying to protect with their bodies the beaten-down wheat that will never be.

Saskatchewan where the farmers, the poor farmers, the small-time farmers who have never made it and never will, let you sleep in their kitchens where the unfinished walls are papered with old newspapers to keep out the terrible cold of winter. Saskatchewan and its flat, clean little cities, where poor men stay drunk in dirty beer parlours. Saskatchewan, bountiful enough to grow wheat for half the masses of China. So tell me, why are your children hungry?

Officially, Saskatchewan is divided into two areas: the largely uninhabited wastelands of the north and the populated prairies of the south. But in reality, a giant arc divides most of the province between poverty and well-being—affluence is probably too strong a word.

The arc begins in the east-central region around Melville and swings north-west, moving just north of Saskatoon and south of North Battleford and over to the Alberta border. On the north side of that line live most of Saskatchewan's rural population. It is also the area of greatest poverty. Within it, there are pockets of even greater depression—which I have written about further on in this chapter. But for the most part, between 40 to 70 per cent of the families on the outside of the arc earn less than $4,000 a year.

It costs money to be a farmer in Saskatchewan today. At very least, you must have assets of $25,000 and product sales of not less than $4,000 a year.

There are approximately 80,000 farm operators today in Saskatchewan, as opposed to 142,390 in 1936. Farms have gotten bigger and more mechanized; the average farm size is 700 acres. But that's only a statistic. In the days when there was a market for wheat, a farm had to be at least 1,000 acres to be economically feasible. Those farms are mainly within the southern area of the province where the population is the most sparse. Only 468,327 people are classified as urban dwellers in Saskatchewan, and the heaviest concentration of rural population is in the marginal farm land outside the arc where the poor continue to eke out a living.

In a province with a population of only 955,344 people, welfare spending is now over $20 million. The figures I have been giving are official figures taken from the 1968 Welfare Report, the A.R.D.A. programs, and various provincial briefs prepared by the Canadian Centre for Community Studies. However, I am convinced that they understate the true figures on poverty in Saskatchewan. Consider, for example, the city of Saskatoon, supposedly not a depressed city.

At first glance, it is a pretty campus town, home of the University of Saskatchewan. The streets are treed, and the South Saskatchewan River winds through the city. There is no apparent slum area. Officially, only 544 families, eight per cent of a population of 115,892, are on welfare. In the downtown area there is even the appearance of a building boom. But apply the Economic Council of Canada's standards of poverty to the city–an annual income of $3,500 a year for a family of four–and you find that 25 per cent of the population live on incomes below that figure. This is a city in which an average home costs $185 a month to rent. There are also other indications that all is not well in Saskatoon. The manager of Seaboard Finance says that the average debt of his customers is now somewhere between $3,000 and $4,000, compared with $500 to $1,500 only a year ago. Within an hour's drive of the city, you can find farm families who are living on an annual income of less than $1,200 a year. The number of children in the Saskatoon region alone who are the wards of the provincial welfare department is 576–almost as many as in Regina, the capital, where 630 children are under government wardship.

Saskatoon, like every other city in Canada, has its bitter illustrations of the gulf between the poor and the middle-class ways of life. When I was there in September, 1969, the university student council spent $14,000 on Frosh Week for the entertainment of the first-year students–fun and games which one new student described as "chicken-shit status-seeking." An editorial in the student paper pointed out that only a few hundred dollars of the money had been spent on intellectual programs, and that, considering the times, it would have been more relevant to have spent the budget on bringing in speakers who would have given the new students a realistic appraisal of the society they were about to enter.

Leave Saskatoon, and the images of poverty in Saskatchewan are no longer hidden. They are stark and grim. Go west to North Battleford; only 787 men out of 2,336 male workers make $4,000 a year or more. Clustered around the northern outskirts of the town are the two- and three-room shacks without water or sewage facilities. Go further north through the Indian and Metis communities of Meadow Lake and Green River, where whole villages are unemployed and lucky to be on welfare. The provincial government has a habit of cutting off welfare to the people during the summer, telling them to go out and fish in the fished-out lakes and hunt for the non-existent game in the bush. Or, failing that, the welfare department tells them to leave their homes and compete with the better-educated, better-trained, and more-favoured white workers in the south. Not long ago, Premier Ross Thatcher promised jobs to the first twenty-five people to leave La Loche and come to Regina. One man took him up on it, and Thatcher's staff spent a couple of days trying to find the man a job. Finally the Premier had to create one for him. In those areas, you can walk through the villages and see children who have faces splotched with impetigo and cold sores, the result of malnutrition and lack of hygiene. Go even further north and east to Sandy Bay, and there, incredible as it may sound, in the middle of a vast wilderness, is a terrible slum in which they even report cases of amoebic dysentery, a disease commonly associated with the teeming, overcrowded slums of Asia.

All through this depressed area of Saskatchewan, the problems of alcoholism are deep and profound, and everywhere family structures are crumbling. In Meadow Lake, an abandoned teen-age girl will do anything to get out of the area. She is severely depressed and desperate. A local gang uses her for casual sexual entertainment and forces her to have intercourse with passing strangers.

On the road between Meadow Lake and Green Lake, I met a man who told me he was forced to desert his wife in La Loche so that his family could get welfare. "If I stay with my family, they won't give us welfare, because they say I'm not sick and I can work. But there's no job within 200 miles of La Loche. So I have to run away. Before she can get welfare, she has to charge me with desertion. If I go back, then they cut off the welfare." It is an old story in the north. By the strange reasoning of bureaucracies, if a woman lives with a man but is not legally married to him, she has no trouble getting welfare. The result of this policy in chronically depressed areas where welfare is the only possible source of income is that it destroys family structures and promotes a permanent dependence on welfare departments. I asked the man how he kept himself. He told me that from time to time he found work clearing stones from farmers' fields at piece-work prices that worked out to 60 cents an hour.

In the Prince Albert area of Saskatchewan, there is a labour force of roughly 85,000 and the official unemployment figure is five per cent. Unofficially, government workers will tell you it is closer to 10 per cent with another five per cent who are permanently unemployable, a total of some 12,750 unemployed workers.

The government's attacks on unemployment seem doomed even before they are started. For example, the Prince Albert Manpower organization, which deals with only about 20 per cent of the working force, gives vocational retraining programs, spending thousands of dollars keeping people in school for six months while paying them a working wage, travelling allowance, and support. The exact amount of money spent is not ascertainable, but the supervisor of the Manpower agency in Prince Albert admits that the dropout rate is 60 per cent and that very few men who complete the courses are hired. Local employers told me they wouldn't hire the graduates, firstly, because they were Indians and couldn't be relied upon, and secondly, because they couldn't make money on them as employees. The Manpower official claims that the students in a vocational school don't learn to work competitively. The employers say they are never taught to work efficiently. Whatever the case, a lot of money is being spent for negligible returns. Stewart Conger, director of the NewStart program in Prince Albert, claims that 25 per cent of the hard-core unemployed can be rehabilitated by the program's methods. The NewStart programs were set up by the Saskatchewan government as private companies to teach "life-skills" to the permanently unemployed in an effort to help them out of poverty. By "conservative" estimates, Conger's agency is dealing with about 4,250 people in the area, but, from what I could learn, the agency actually gets to work with only about 100 people a year. And achievements for NewStart have been thin in Saskatchewan. Something like $35,000 has been spent on training teachers' aides and another $25,000 on welfare aides. The thinking was that these people would find employment and simultaneously relieve the professionals of expensive baby-sitting chores. However, teacher organizations and welfare workers have resisted the idea, mainly on the grounds that their professional structures were being infiltrated by uneducated and untrained people who would lower the status of their professions.

About an hour west of Prince Albert, the social worker turns the car north off the paved highway and onto a gravel road. The countryside here doesn't have the majestic, rolling sweep of the prairies just a few miles further south. The wheat fields here skirt islands of heavy bush and short stands of scrubby poplar. The lands further south border the North Saskatchewan River, and the soil there is rich and black. Here it is poor; "degraded black soil" is the technical term. There are stone piles everywhere. Formerly grassland, later invaded by brush, the soil has been leached of its acid content; it hasn't the organic matter or plant nutrients needed for successful farming. All over Saskatchewan, the people have been leaving the land since the 1930's. But in this particular area, the exodus was twice as great as that from any other rural part of the province. Just a few miles north-west, the land is vacant, abandoned. It is easy to understand why the people leave. This marginal land must have broken the hearts of the most enthusiastic men and women. And there is an oppressive air of desolation, a brooding quality to the land that is almost palpable. All the natural surroundings seem to conspire to make humans alien to the landscape. The people are silent, suspicious, turned in upon themselves, as if contemplating their own self-destruction. It was in this area a few months ago that a young man went berserk, shooting to death nine members of a farm family.

The few people that are left here struggle against a poverty as inexorable as a treadmill. It is as if they are caught in a dark, narrow tunnel in which they cannot even turn around, but in which they must toil unknowingly toward some dismal end. Although something like 60 per cent of the land is used for farming, and it is still the most widespread form of employment, almost 70 per cent of the farms have total product sales below $3,750, and almost 60 per cent have capital assets of less than $25,000. According to the 1964 A.R.D.A. standards, those two figures form the dividing line between rural poverty and rural well-being. If a farmer is in the "low income" bracket, where his gross sales are $3,750 a year, his net income can be arrived at by deducting the accepted 50 per cent agricultural overhead. In other words, at least 70 per cent of the farm families in this area of Saskatchewan are realizing a net income of less than $1,875 a year. For those in search of a Canadian Appalachia, it is here, west of Prince Albert, Saskatchewan.

By now the dust from the gravel road is seeping through the door-jamb of the car and hanging in a haze in front of the dashboard. The social worker curses, coughs the dust out of his throat, and spits out the window. He is young, in his late twenties. This is his province. He grew up north of Saskatoon, went away to school and came back. Why, he doesn't really know. Like most welfare workers in this province, he is defensive and bitter: "Sure welfare workers are

97

stupid. They're really idiots. Because they've bitten off more than they can chew. There is not one-tenth of the money available to do what they know should be done in social welfare, and yet they allow themselves to be conned into attempting programs on that 10 per cent budget. Then they allow themselves to be judged by their failure." He spits out of the window again in disgust. But he is a good guy. If his superiors ever found out that I was with him today, or that he took me where we are going, he would probably be fired. The annual turnover among the field staff in the Saskatchewan welfare departments is fantastic. Department heads will privately admit that it is "something like 50 per cent," but the social workers themselves claim it is closer to 100 per cent.

We turn into a farm that is set back from the road. The house is weathered, unpainted. Missing window panes have been covered over with scraps of plywood. Three neglected-looking children are playing in the yard as we drive up. They stand silent, watching. From a stoop at the back of the house, a woman is hanging up her wash. She looks like one of the stunted trees of this region. Even though she has just done her washing, her fingernails are still black. The knuckles are swollen and twisted. The flecks of soap on her forearms contrast against the dark, sinewy flesh. She has a drawn, exhausted face, and it seems as if everything feminine or human has long since been drained out of her. The social worker later told me she was forty-two; she looked at least sixty. Only when I looked into her face, I saw that she still had soft brown eyes. They were sympathetic and intelligent. She must have been a young woman with hope and dreams at one time, who never thought she would ever have to struggle like this to keep what was left of her family together. Her husband disappeared six months ago. Her eldest boy, who is eighteen, is in trouble with the law. She and her three younger children are living on an emergency welfare budget of $146 a month. And now her niece has come to stay with her. She is her dead sister's girl and only fifteen years of age. Ostensibly, she has come to help, but the girl has some terrible problems of her own.

After some awkward introductions, the social worker tells the woman as matter-of-factly as he can that her son has been sent away for six months, but there are still some outstanding charges of car theft against him for which he has yet to be prosecuted. She says nothing, continuing to hang up her clothes with nervous, bird-like movements. The social worker goes on to talk about other things. Now that the winter is approaching, he is trying to get her to accept the idea of moving into the city, even though he knows the accommodations she will be able to afford on welfare won't be any better than what she has now. But at least she won't be so isolated. The woman doesn't want to leave the farm, you can see that. She is clinging to the few things she has left. She thinks her husband will come back here, but even as she says it, her face shows she doesn't really believe he will. And she is worried about her children. "They'll grow away from me in the city," she says. "That's what happened to my eldest boy. He went to work there, now look what they've done to him." The social worker discusses something else and goes on to suggest that she apply for an additional clothing allowance. Then we go looking for her niece. The girl is on the front porch, and, as we go to walk around the house, I glance back. The woman is sitting on the back stoop, rocking gently, her hands closed tightly over her knees. She is silent, but the tears are running down her cheeks.

The porch must have been screened in at one time, but the mesh is broken and sagging and the screen door hangs permanently open on one hinge. The girl is a plain, pathetic, little creature with a thin, white face. Her shoulders are hunched forward, her arms crossed over her stomach as if to hide her pregnancy. Her eyes dart nervously away from ours. The social worker tries to talk with her, but it's impossible, and the conversation is reduced to his questions and her whispered, monosyllabic answers. He tells her that in another month she will have to go to one of the Salvation Army homes for unwed mothers in Prince Albert or Saskatoon, and that the government will pay for her keep for three months before the baby is born and two months after. He also tries to explain to her that she has been made a temporary ward of the province and that her baby will also be a ward until formally adopted. The social worker is a nice guy, and he is trying to explain it all as gently and patiently as possible. But the girl is terrified. I leave and wait for him by the car. After a while he comes over. He is tired and depressed and before getting in the car, he lights a cigarette.

"Where's the boyfriend in all this?" I ask.

He gives me a strange look. "There is no boyfriend. It's her father. The son-of-a-bitch has been doing her for a couple of years, ever since her mother died. When she got pregnant, he threw her out. The aunt has told me all this, but they're both so scared of the girl's father we can't get them to give us a statement."

"But . . . ."

"But what? Don't worry, I've tried everything. I even tackled him with it. He told me he thought incest in some cases was permissible, because, after all, it was right there in the Bible. Anyway," he continued, "the problem now is how do you go about salvaging a kid like that?"

As we drove out of the farmyard, I caught one last glimpse of her. She was sitting in the same position, staring out at a future that held nothing.

In 1968, the Saskatchewan government had almost 3,400 children under twenty-one in its care; 1,400 were Indian and Metis. More than 1,000 children a year between the ages of twelve to seventeen come under the government's care. The total number of illegitimate births in the province last year was almost 3,000–there was even one borne by a twelve-year-old white girl. But 35 per cent of the mothers were Indian and Metis, even though, as an ethnic group, they form less than eight per cent of the population.

There is, of course, no public record of the number of incestuous births among the poor, among whom it is not so much a sexual aberration as it is an index of the family disintegration that results from poverty. But enough evidence exists to indicate that the reports one hears from the social workers and from the Indian and Metis families in the north are more than paranoid fiction from the oppressed mind. I have seen the documented evidence that a former psychiatric social worker doing research work at the North Battleford mental hospital and now a guidance counsellor in the Winnipeg school system, took time to gather together. It often happens that young Indian and Metis girls are subject to sexual exploitation–"rape," you might call it–in the foster homes in which they are placed by various welfare agencies. Even the most blatant examples of abuse, however, are difficult to prove, and, even if it were possible, the libel laws of this country would prevent their publication. But white society will one day pay for turning a blind eye to this most vicious form of racism. When the researcher took the evidence he had gathered to the local authorities in North Battleford, he was illegally detained by the police. (The North Battleford police force was replaced by the R.C.M.P. shortly after this incident.) When the same man acted on his own initiative to get Indian children out of homes in which they were being sexually abused, he lost his job for crossing inter-departmental barriers.

One of the ever-present ironies of our society is that those who work in the institutions charged with the responsibility of social welfare are quickly rendered helpless and powerless if they question any of the inflexible policies of those institutions. In turn, they become victims of those same policies. It is small surprise then that social workers, in order to survive, quickly become faceless machines, mere instruments of inhuman bureaucracies.

There are other, more apparent aspects of racism in Saskatchewan. Although the Indian and Metis compose only 7.5 to eight per cent of the population, proportionately ten times more of them are jailed in comparison with the white population. They make up 74 per cent of those jailed for liquor offences in the provincial jails of Regina and Prince Albert. In the federal jail at Prince Albert, Indian and Metis constitute 38 per cent of the inmates. In the Prince Albert women's jail, 90 per cent of the inmates are Indian and Metis. And why, asks Dr. Howard Adams of the University of Saskatchewan, why in a place like La Loche, where there are only jobs for a dozen men, is the provincial government planning to spend $100,000 on building a local jail?

In the park at 14th and 102nd in North Battleford, there are groups of children playing or walking idly around the trees and equipment. It is a soft fall day, and the first leaves of the hardwood trees are beginning to turn yellow. In the centre of the park, a group of older boys and girls, between the ages of fifteen and seventeen, are playing some kind of tug-of-war game. At first glance, it seems light-hearted, but then it gets rougher as two Metis boys whirl the girls around in a circle. The three white girls break off and walk away, being teased for a while by the two boys. When the girls get far enough away, one of them turns back and yells, "Hey, you. You're a stupid shit!"

The two boys had gone back to talk to an Indian girl, but now they turn around, quiet. The Indian girl, moving in a strange circle of self-denigration and provocation, yells back, "Why don't you call them stupid Indian shits?"

The white girl complies. It is silent in the park; the other groups of children are listening. Here and there, some adults are standing, watching. One of the boys is shirtless. Dark and very lean, he lifts himself up on his toes and yells across the grass, "Hey, you! I'm going to fuck you!"

You can almost see the words moving across the park, penetrating the sensuous green air, peeling back the membranes that cover the swollen little cancers of race hatred. Like a slow-moving projectile, the words leave little shock waves behind, and, as they spread out, you can see the adults stirring, as if ruffling feathers, looking around at each other.

The Metis boy breaks the tension by leaping forward and sprinting after the white girl. She panics and comes pounding across the turf. What are you running from, white girl? Juggling your books under one arm, fat white knees pumping hard. In no time he has caught her. She stops, her face red and heavy. She swings her purse in a circle to ward him off. For a minute he stays, watching, enjoying her fear. Then, laughing in delight, he spins around and runs back to his companion. Together they race off to a beaten-up Chevy that is crumbling with rust. Then they're gone.

A few yards away, a white-haired old man is shaking his head. There are red splotches on his pale face. He is both angry and excited; it's not every afternoon you get action like that in North Battleford.

"If the cops had been here," he says, "them two Indians would be on the way to the cells by now."

"Yes," I say, "I guess you're right about that."

7

Keeping the Poor That Way

There is a curious vein of hypocrisy underlying the official recognition that poverty exists in this country. Curious because those who are publicly demanding that something be done about the inequities of our system are often the ones making the most money from the conditions that exist. And much of what continues to be done in the administration of business, politics, law, education, and all the other institutions that form the working machinery of society, has the net effect of keeping the poor that way.

For example, the worst crisis facing the poor and most working-class Canadians is the lack of adequate housing. And yet the real-estate and land speculators continue to make enormous and uncontrolled profits—all the while piously stating that "we must roll up our sleeves and go to work to help the poor help themselves."

Canadian real-estate developers do not have much to be proud of. In the past twenty-five years, they have had an almost free hand in putting together parcels of land. They have ringed the cities with impossible suburbs, all in the pursuit of enormous personal profits—largely tax exempt. The developers can be cursed for much of the chaos that is presently killing the large cities. So it was a refreshing change to hear Thomas N. Shea, outgoing president of the Ontario Association of Real-Estate Boards, bring the Economic Council of Canada's report on poverty to the attention of the 400 delegates attending the Association's 47th annual conference held early in 1969 at Windsor. "We must rid ourselves," said Shea, "of the archaic notions that poverty represents only the lack of essentials to sustain life . . . it also includes the insufficient access not only to shelter – the item we are most concerned with – but also to decency, pride, and acceptance into our so-called 'Just Society'." He went on to call on all Canadians to solve "the people problems" that face the country today – but he never mentioned that many had "insufficient access" to a decent house because of the stranglehold so many real-estate developers have on prime land. Mr. Shea's own company, which is a real-estate agency, is most active in Markham, on the north-eastern outskirts of Toronto, and the local papers in that district carried excerpts from Mr. Shea's speech (real-estate firms are big advertisers). As if to unconsciously underline the irony of Mr. Shea's statements, one of the newspapers also carried in the same issue the report of how a man living in the same district had been sentenced to eighteen months in jail. The man, an out-of-work truck driver, had spent the winter living in a chicken house in the neighbouring village of Green River with his wife and their seven children. The family had attempted to get emergency housing but had been rebuffed by officials. They survived on casual welfare handouts. He was imprisoned for defrauding local store-owners with a series of six false cheques, which totalled just over $100 – not one of them was for more than $30. The cheques had been cashed to buy food for his family. It is true that the man had been in trouble with the law before, and he had served time in jail. It is also true that the district court judge who sentenced him at Whitby held off sending him to jail for two months on the condition that he find a job. However, nobody in Mr. Shea's Markham community would give him a job, nor did anyone come forward with some alternative temporary housing for the family. The children were split up in several welfare homes. A year later they finally got together again. It only remains to point out that the community must have been aware of what was happening: some weeks before Mr. Shea made his Windsor speech, the man's predicament was reported not only in the local papers but also in the big metropolitan Toronto dailies, which, however, did not follow the story long enough to report that the man had been imprisoned.

So there, in microcosm, is an example of the conditions which permit poverty to thrive in this country. A leading member of the business community makes a ringing speech about confronting poverty—an obvious situation exists where something could be done—the newspapers exploit the obvious and sensational aspects of the incident. In the end, nothing is done. And it is left to the courts to sweep the problem away where it won't be seen. Out of desperation, a man steals $100, and society puts him away, even though it costs $5,000 a year to keep him in prison. But more importantly he is kept the way he is, in poverty.

Perhaps it demands too much of idealism to hope that the principals in the incident above might have acted differently, but there are many more, all-too-similar examples. For instance, in September, Liberal M.P. Robert Kaplan organized a special seminar at which his constituents of Don Valley and others were invited to discuss the problems confronting big cities. The seminar dealt with overcrowding, housing, noise and other urban problems. Now Mr. Kaplan married into the Tanenbaum family, which owns the York construction company and the Runnymede land development company, each with an estimated $50 million in assets, partly in land holdings in Pickering, Brock, and Markham townships. Kaplan's election campaign was one of the most expensive in the country. Declared costs were $68,917, (after all, he did beat Dalton Camp, a formidable political opponent) but that figure would not normally include sums that may have been spent by others on his behalf. One assumes that land developers were canvassed for his campaign fund.

A noteworthy example of the manner in which housing problems are created relates to the Rubin Corporation. On March 13, 1969 it applied for and obtained permission from the property committee of the Etobicoke Board of Education to build a low-rental project for the Ontario Housing Corporation. However, it appeared that there were some flaws with the site. First, the ten acres were the property of a sewer-pipe manufacturer and were classified as industrial land. Lying east of Burlington Street in the former town of Mimico, the site is bounded on three sides by a truck route, a C.N.R. trunk-line, and more industrial wasteland. Secondly, the committee pointed out, adequate educational facilities existed for a project of no more than 150 units. However, presumably to make a substantial profit, the Rubin Corporation obtained the O.H.C.'s agreement in multiplying the optimum density by four, to build 620 units. For the 524 children who would be housed in such a complex, it would probably mean a school would have to be built for them, further isolating the low-rental project from the world outside. "It is the worst possible site," said Trustee Nora Pownall. She pointed out that with such a population density, the project was destined to become a ghetto even before it was built. It is only more evidence of the middle-class dictating the terms under which they think the poor should live.

In March, 1969, the Central Mortgage and Housing Corporation produced a report which showed that during the previous year there had been a considerable building boom—but only for the rich. The report showed that the families in the lower third of the income strata—those earning less than $5,751 a year—made up only 6.5 per cent of all borrowers under the National Housing Act, legislation that was created specifically for low-income groups. In Toronto, where the housing shortage for low-income groups is of emergency proportions, only 2.7 per cent of borrowers were in the under-$6,000-a-year class. Just under one-half of borrowers came from middle-income groups and 44.1 per cent from the upper third. There were other discrepancies; families with over four children made up only 11.5 per cent of borrowers, while those without children made up 25 per cent. Families in low-income brackets who somehow managed to borrow money from the N.H.A. undoubtedly got themselves into trouble. Government agencies have set a ceiling of 27 per cent of family income that can be used to pay for shelter. (In Western European socialist countries, the ceiling is between eight and 12 per cent.) However, to afford an N.H.A. mortgage and stay within the 27 per cent limit, a family would have to make $8,000 a year; a family which made, say, $4,000 a year, would have to devote 38.3 per cent of its income to paying off the mortgage.

The C.M.H.C. also reported that the minimum income necessary to qualify for a maximum N.H.A. loan over a forty-year term was $9,970. This salary would be needed to pay back a $25,000 loan at 9.25 per cent interest.

In the off-again, on-again freeze that has hampered real progress in the area of public housing, it was estimated that in March, 1969, the number of Ontario projects caught by the federal government's vacillation amounted to forty-five separate programs valued at $38.5 million. This amounted to homes for more than 3,000 families. But even so, it is a drop in the bucket when compared to what is required. In Toronto alone, there is a demand for at least 4,000 units a year. The Metropolitan Planning Board issued a report on May 21, 1969, that called for a minimum of 35,000 public housing units by 1981 at a cost of $560 million. Even if this goal were met, it would only take care of "the most severe hardship needs," the report explained. It would still leave 182,200 families in the metropolitan area inadequately housed. More than 8,000 families have put their names down on the waiting list. Of these, 3,325 were single female heads of households. Because the Ontario Housing Corporation, the government-subsidized agency, has a rule that limits such families to 30 per cent of the population in its projects, there are at present only 1,907 female heads of households living in subsidized housing. In other words, if you're poor and your husband has run out on you, then you have even less chance of getting a decent house than if you're poor and still have a husband.

These figures do not represent a sudden demand. As far back as 1965, Robert Bradley, then the director of the Toronto City Housing Authority, pointed out that although 4,000 families desperately needed houses that year, the city built only fifty-four units. "Parents," he said, "have been driven to putting out their children for adoption rather than jam them into rotting rooms in Cabbage Town."

On April, 12, 1969, a study released by Patterson Planning and Research Ltd. showed that 113,000 families in metropolitan Toronto were living in housing beyond their means. Another 60,000 families lived in overcrowded quarters, and an additional 48,000 occupied accommodations that were both inadequate and too expensive.

Let us take a look at some of the rather feeble attempts made by government in 1969 to help low-income wage earners find decent housing, a right the Hellyer Task Force On Housing described as basic to the Canadian way of life. On June 24, the Conservative Ontario government of John Robarts announced that it was willing to pump $50 million into second mortgages to make home-ownership easier for those in the $6,000-to-$10,000-a-year income bracket. The idea was that if you made $7,500 a year, you could put $750 down and pay $174 a month for a house. However, there was a catch to this largesse. The plan would only apply to homes that cost no more than $19,000. Now, it is possible to find a home in Ontario for $19,000, and if you went far enough into the countryside, you might even find one selling for $10,000. But the housing crisis is not in the countryside. It is in metropolitan Toronto. And as Don Kirkup, research director for the Toronto Real-Estate Board pointed out, "the plan is entirely irrelevant for single family detached homes in Metro, where the average cost of a new detached house is $35,118." Even semi-detached new homes in Metro cost over $30,000. The only type of new home the $19,000 price would possibly cover would be a condominium, but, as Jack Hurlburt, head of the public relations committee of the Toronto Home Builders' Association observed, there was just no reasonably priced land available for condominium housing. And by the fall of 1969, the average price of a condominium home had risen to $24,000. By October, 1969, the Ontario government had to admit that "not a nickel" of the $50 million had been used. Provincial Cabinet Minister Stanley Randall blamed Ottawa, saying the federal government's tight-money policies had made it impossible for home buyers to borrow down payments from banks and loan companies.

The Ontario government had moved on other fronts. Earlier in the year, they had passed legislation that would speed up the machinery of expropriation. In August, 1969, the Robarts government announced that legislation was in the works that would allow municipalities to expropriate private property for the use of large commercial land developers. The reaction of the small home-owner to this new legislation was best articulated by Raymond P. Brown, president of the Bedford Park Home-owners' Association, in this letter to the Toronto *Star*:

> When we passed the new laws in Ontario dealing with the expropriation of property a few months ago, it was not hard to guess what would be the sequel to it, and we have not had long to wait.
>
> It has just been announced that the government of Ontario contemplates legislation that will enable municipalities to expropriate property for wealthy business enterprises on the grounds that it is for the public good. In other words, they are considering a law that would enable big businesses to take the property of the small home-owners and use it to enlarge their holdings; strictly a take-from-the-poor-and-give-to-the-rich program.
>
> For the government to take private property for the public good such as schools, hospitals, roads and so on, is a principle that is understood and accepted. To take property from one private citizen to give it to another private citizen is an outrage.

But it is not an isolated outrage. I want to show how this attitude permeates all the other private and public institutions that are the operating machinery of this society. In the brief list that follows, there are examples that range from political administration through education to the law.

In new industrial development: when Senator Edgar Fournier (P.C., New Brunswick) appeared on May 20, 1969, before the Senate's special committee on poverty, he pointed out that new industry for depressed areas was not necessarily a cure-all for poverty. He pointed out that when a $100-million power plant was being constructed in the Mactaquac region of New Brunswick, supported with some $21 million of federal funds, there was a small Indian village only a stone's throw from the dam where the people were living in extreme poverty. But during the construction, not one person out of the fifty families in the village was given a job.

In political administration: after the British Columbia elections in August, 1969, Premier W. A. C. Bennett claimed that he had once again saved British Columbia and the rest of Canada from socialism. However, the poor in that province have paid a high price for "the good life," the Social Credit slogan which apparently describes the life-style of the rest of the province's citizens. For in British Columbia, there are 40,000 family heads registered on welfare, representing almost 100,000 people. It has been estimated that at least 20,000 could be "rehabilitated." Questioned about this, Mr. Bennett says that welfare systems have never worked well and never will. Strangely, for a conservative, he thinks the solution is a negative income tax which would grant people a guaranteed minimum income. Mr. Bennett's government has even gone so far as initiating a study of such a program. But the study is described by Mr. Bennett as an aid to the federal government in designing minimum income legislation, which he says, could be implemented only by Ottawa and not by his own government.

Also in the area of political administration, in the first week of May, 1969, it was revealed in the Ontario legislature during a debate of spending estimates that although $1.3 million had been appropriated by the government for spending on Indian development in the province during 1968, only $300,000 had been used. Pressed for an explanation by the Opposition leaders in the house, John Yaremko, Minister of Social and Family Services, admitted that there was really no legal problem preventing the province from assisting the Indians with the money—it was just that it was difficult to get joint financial agreements from Ottawa on spending programs. "How long do you expect the Indians to wait for you?" shouted Liberal leader Robert Nixon. "They've waited a hundred years already!"

Under the Minimum Wage Act: on April 15, 1969, the executive director of the Ontario Labour Department's Manpower Services, Michael Warren, revealed that Ontario employers were guilty of cheating Indians, the poor, the unskilled, and new immigrants at the rate of $100,000 a month in contravention of provincial legislation requiring a minimum wage of $1.30 an hour. He said that during the first three months of the year, over a quarter of a million dollars had been collected from 1,700 employers who had been underpaying a total of 10,736 workers. Warren admitted there was no way to tell how many other employers were getting away with the cheating or even of counting those who paid up voluntarily as soon as they were confronted by their employees. During the year, he expected the department would be called on to force employers to pay up more than a million dollars. He said that the most common excuse offered was, "these people aren't worth any more . . . we are really doing them a favour by employing them." One case involved a construction company in north-western Ontario which not only refused its twenty-three Indian employees the minimum wage and vacation pay but in some cases paid its employees in groceries instead of cash. Another case involved a large private hospital which cheated its fifty-seven female employees out of $9,974 under the equal-pay-for-equal-work law. Mr. Warren observed that he didn't think that, even when paid, the minimum wage of $1.30 an hour was an adequate or fair salary. "It's a minimum standard," he said, "to protect employees from exploitation." Nevertheless, some 200,000 Ontario workers are estimated to exist on the minimum wage.

In the administration of education: in answer to a question from Paul Yewchuk (P.C., Athabaska), it was revealed in the House of Commons on July 7, 1969, that during the 1967-68 fiscal year, the federal government had contributed $7.2 million to the post-secondary education of foreign students in Canada—$4,320,000 of that amount, more than half, was spent on foreign undergraduate students. By comparison, during the same period, the government spent $312,603 for the post-secondary education of Canadian Indians and Eskimos. Of this amount, $311,103 was spent at the undergraduate level.

Ontario Liberal M.P.P. Tim Reid prepared a special paper for the Liberal policy conference held in August, 1969, at the University of Guelph. In it, he pointed out that the technology of education was already freezing conditions in society to prevent children of low-income families from progressing upwards, something parents of poor children have known for a long time. A group of mothers in the Trefann Court area of Toronto made a year-long study of the kind of education their children were receiving: they concluded that many of the so-called "opportunity classes" their children were pushed into were nothing more than dead ends, and that the decisions to put them there were made not so much on the basis of intelligence as on economic background. The classes teach such skills as basic wood-working, baby-sitting, and muffin-making, which is all that is available to children who have learning problems in school and who live in the slum areas of large cities. One mother, Noreen Gaudette, forty-eight, a life-time resident of the area, said children were brainwashed into believing they could do no better.

The most damning evidence weighed against education for the poor and disadvantaged was given in June, 1969, by Walter Currie, an Indian and the regional director of Ontario provincial schools. He pointed out that the education system seems to be set up to punish Indian children for being what they are. "At some schools," he said, "children are physically punished for speaking their own language–which, in some cases, is the only one they know." The result, he said, is that only thirty-five Treaty Indians–less than three per cent of those who started in Grade One–are in Grade Thirteen in Ontario.

On the preference for international expositions: on September 15, 1968, a number of delegates at a conference on poverty in Montreal put forth statistics which showed that more than half of the city's population lived under what were described as "intolerable financial conditions." One speaker, G. Roland Hennessey, assistant executive director of the Federation of Catholic Charities, said that a third of the population could be described as destitute in 1966, as compared to 27 per cent in 1946. He said 38 per cent of Montrealers now live in abject poverty, privation, and misery. Other statistics showed that in April, 1968, more than 11,000 Montreal families lived on incomes of less than $1,000 per annum. Hennessey said that 27 per cent of the housing in the inner city was fit only for immediate demolition. Obviously, whatever profits came into the province because of Expo were never available for use by the poor.

On preference for meeting rooms: on August 14, 1969, Robert Andras, the federal cabinet minister in charge of housing policies, stated that the government's freeze on urban renewal and low-income housing projects would continue indefinitely, at least up to a year.

In the beginning of September, the federal cabinet gave

official compliance to spending $600,000 to renovate the old Ottawa Union Station, which is scheduled for eventual demolition. The renovated station would be used as temporary accommodation for future federal-provincial conferences. Previous conferences had been held in the Confederation Room in the West Block on Parliament Hill.

In the area of municipal administration: Store Creek divides the Northern Ontario community of Moosonee. On one side live 400 whites, with hydro, sewers, running water, and garbage barrels marked "Keep Moosonee Clean." On the other side live 1,000 Indians in 125 houses that are without all those modern amenities. On June 14, 1969, the destitute Indians of Moosonee sent an open letter to their fellow citizens of Ontario, asking for donations of plastic garbage bags so they could organize their own garbage collection services.

The list is endless, and, as can be seen, these are not isolated incidents of neglect that could be attributed to administrative oversight; they are, in fact, the overriding policies of political, private, and bureaucratic institutions.

In the area of Indian administration: probably one of the most frustrating areas for any well-intentioned and dedicated person to work in is that administrative no-man's land between the Indians of this country and the various levels of federal, provincial, and municipal government. In the spring of 1969, Joseph Dufour, director of the Indian Development Branch of the Ontario Department of Family and Social Services, resigned from his $16,000-a-year job. So did six of his nine co-workers. There was no doubting the sincerity of Dufour's action and those of his co-workers, because in the days that followed, they detailed with great honesty and bluntness the political gamesmanship that had thwarted many of their attempts to help the 90,000 Indians in Ontario. In a series of articles, interviews, and television appearances, Dufour made some very telling points.

His main argument was that his department, the Indian Development Branch, had been made impotent by being continually denied the authority to spend money on valid Indian projects, money that had been officially allocated by the government for such use. His budget was made up of an annual $1 million for expenditures under a provincial-federal agreement, and $4 million annually for administrative costs. He was never able to use even half of it.

When, in 1968, the federal government began its discussions of revising the Indian Act, one of the largest Indian organizations, the Union of Ontario Indians, realized that most Indians didn't even know what the Indian Act was all about. So they thought it would be a good idea if someone would go out and explain the Act to the people on the reservations. They asked Dufour for a $10,000 grant to do so. He in turn recommended the grant, but it was refused by senior officials in the department of Family and Social Services on the pretext that there were no funds available for such causes, even though, as Dufour pointed out, "We were sitting on a million dollars."

For some time, university students of Indian background had been sponsored by the National Indian Youth Council to attend summer seminars at various universities in different provinces. One seminar was to be held in 1968 at an Ontario university, and the National Indian Youth Council asked if Dufour's department would contribute $1,000 toward the costs of the six-week seminar. Dufour was again refused, this time on the grounds that the money was not for excursions.

For some time, one of the most urgent Indian problems has been the Indian's first and often disastrous contact with big city life. Dufour's department, the Social Planning Coun-

cil of Metropolitan Toronto, the Indian-Eskimo Association, the federal government's Indian Affairs Branch, and the Canadian Indian Centre decided after some discussion that one of the best contributions they could make would be to turn a researcher loose on this specific problem for a year. The budgeted cost: $7,000. Once again, Dufour was told the funds were not available. Dufour also went through the bureaucratic run-around which reveals the jealousy and ill-will held against his department by officials in the Family and Social Services Branch. His staff spent hours preparing various guideline papers that were asked for by senior officials, but meetings to discuss the papers and projects were never afterwards held. As Dufour said in a television news interview, "How could I keep going back empty-handed to the Indians, and then ask them to believe we were sincere in our desire to help them?"

In the administration of the law: it is not only the Indian who has a rough time when he first hits the big city. If you are poor and a stranger and get into trouble with the law in Toronto, the odds are that you are in for a very rough time. Take, for example, the case of young Derek Green from Newfoundland. Charged in the summer of 1969 with theft, possession of stolen goods, and public mischief, his trial date was set and bail was established at $500. As a *Globe and Mail* editorial writer pointed out, it might have been $5 million. Green was remanded and spent forty-four days in the dilapidated Don Jail. Remanded for another week, he went berserk in the courtroom and then tried to hang himself.

Green was later found guilty and imprisoned. But as Professor Martin Friedman pointed out in his book *Detention Before Trial*, there is abundant evidence to indicate that the criteria used to judge whether or not a man is freed on his own recognizance are usually involved with his personal wealth. This system is maintained even though the courts are daily full of examples in which citizens are jailed, only to be found innocent or found guilty, fined, and then set free. Canada, as it has been said over and over again, imprisons more people per capita than any other democratic country in the western world. This is surely one indicator of the punitive attitude held by our legal and judicial institutions.

It is also interesting to note that while the legal establishment has attempted to introduce a more equitable legal aid system, it has also seen that the profession is very well taken care of. The legal aid program in Ontario began March 13, 1967. It uses public funds to pay the legal fees of people who can't afford to hire their own lawyers. The lawyers charge 75 per cent of the regular fee. It seems fairly safe to assume that justice for the poor hardly existed before 1967, because the cost of the program in the first year was over $4 million, more than double the original estimate; in its second year, the program cost over $7 million. The public money for legal aid is administered by the Law Society of Upper Canada, which in fact means the legal profession has a new multi-million dollar pie to slice up among its members. As Horace Krever, former law professor at the University of Toronto, told the Ontario Welfare Council's annual conference at Hart House on May 14, 1969, "The plan makes sure the rights of lawyers are put foremost." Krever suggested that the legal aid program be taken out of the hands of lawyers and placed under the control of the community, which, after all, pays for it.

In treatment of the elderly: at the far end of the age scale is the repressive attitude our society has toward the elderly. One in ten Canadians is over sixty-five, says the John S. Morgan School of Social Work at the University of Toronto, and half of them are living in poverty. In Ontario, the wealthiest province in Canada, there are 56,000 men and women over fifty living on welfare, and thousands are barely surviving. On June 17, 1969, Miss Ethel Neilson, who is eighty-one, presented a brief to Health Minister John Munro which documented that many pensioners had to buy cat and dog foods to stay alive. One of the most frightening realities to face in this country is to be old and poor with nowhere to go. For the six subsidized homes for the aged run by the Metro Toronto Housing Department, there are waiting lists of eighteen months or more. The old people have literally to wait for someone to die before they can find accommodation. In the meantime, they have to fend for themselves. And I can think of no more appropriate way of ending this chapter than to include the opening sentence of Miss Neilson's brief to Health Minister Munro: "You know, of course, that nobody can live on $109.10 a month in Canada today." That is the pittance which is the current old-age pension.

Keeping the Rich That Way

The middle-class writers of this country never seem able to make up their minds whether to slap our wrists for our "spiteful anti-Americanism" or to fan the flames of nationalism to a more intense heat.

I know that for much of what is in this chapter I will certainly be labelled anti-American. It is an irrelevent accusation. Because what I have to say here is argued on the premise that if we are to ever overcome poverty in our country, we must come to understand much more than we now know of how the rich and corporate few who do rule over us come to power and how they keep it. In this area there is still much investigating to be done. But the first step in this direction is to understand the degree of American control over the finances of our nation; in this regard, we are in no better a position than Peru–despite Foreign Minister Mitchell Sharp's wafflings.

If you think the comparison between ourselves and the Peruvians is an extravagant one, then let me point out that Ferdinand Lundberg, in his scholarly tome *The Rich and the Super Rich*, points out that a majority of American citizens labour under the economic oppression usually associated with the benevolent oligarchy of a Latin American "banana republic." Most "affluent" Canadians, like the majority of "affluent" Americans, own little more than the clothes on their backs, a car, and a few other shiny gadgets which they have been led to believe are the symbols of economic success. Despite the well-worn democratic mythology that pervades both countries, very few citizens have any involvement in the real wealth or power of the United States and Canada. The possibility that in this country they ever can or ever will is decreasing rapidly.

In 1964, foreigners owned $33 billion worth of assets in Canada, while Canadians owned only $13 billion worth of assets abroad. Payments of interest and dividends to foreigners is now over $1 billion a year. These figures are from the report of the Task Force on the structure of Canadian industry, better known as the Watkins Report.

To continue, in 1963 foreigners controlled 97 per cent of the capital employed in the manufacture of automobiles and parts, 97 per cent in rubber, 78 per cent in chemicals, and 77 per cent in electrical apparatus. American control in these areas was, respectively, 97 per cent, 90 per cent, 54 per cent, and 66 per cent.

"By any criterion," writes Gabriel Kolko, professor of history at New York State University, in his book *The Roots of American Foreign Policy,* "what we call United States investment abroad is much more foreign resources mobilized in American hands, generating its own capital in a manner that pyramids the American penetration of the world economy. Whatever else they may be, profits on such investments are not primarily the reward for the transfer of American capital abroad."

To which it is only necessary to add what former u.s. Secretary of State John Foster Dulles once said: "There are

123

two ways to gain control of a nation. One is to gain control of its people by force. The other is to gain control of its economy by financial means."

That our own élites have aided and abetted the United States in winning this control is revealed by another fact from the Watkins Report: "The most serious deficiency has been the training of top management with consequent deleterious effects on the quality of Canadian entrepreneurship. The gap in formal education of the managers of Canadian firms, relative to U.S. firms, is greater than in any other occupational group."

This statement is borne out by the fact that, by 1963, Canadians were paying a total of $245 million a year to foreigners—in royalties, franchise payments, advertising, rent, professional fees—for the privilege of showing us how to sell-out our own national wealth.

The report also showed that of the 414 corporations which held assets of more than $25 million in 1963, at least 50 per cent of those assets were controlled by non-residents. That the United States was not interested in the smaller corporations is demonstrated in the fact that of those firms with less than $25 million in assets, only 32 per cent of the total capital was in foreign hands. Of total taxable corporate income in 1965, 18 per cent was earned by 130 of the largest private corporations—most of which were in foreign hands.

There are many indications that foreign ownership and control of the Canadian economy have increased enormously since 1963. The figures for that year showed foreign control of Canadian manufacturing to be 54 per cent, of mining and smelting 59 per cent, and of petroleum and natural gas 74 per cent. In the twenty months following the Watkins Report, another 500 Canadian companies have been taken over by American firms.

What then of the Canadian government, standing on the

sidelines, influenced by powerful lobby groups in the Senate, involved with myriad corporate directorships—what of the millionaire Liberal M.P.'s, fighting for the "privacy of industry"?

Well, the Economic Council of Canada had the temerity in its *Sixth Annual Report* to say that we had little control of our inflationary problems because the control measures really rested in the hands of United States government and business. And when the Council argued that far from helping, the measures enacted by the Trudeau government would only cause higher unemployment and possibly a damaging recession, then the Liberal Cabinet became quite upset. There was much talk in Ottawa that the Council should be reshuffled, perhaps to include more specialists who might come up with analyses which would follow more closely the government guidelines. Shades of Peru? or Brazil? Or shades, perhaps, of Premier Joey Smallwood, who didn't like the bleak economic outlook reported by his own government commission in 1969 —so he dismissed it and hired a New York public relations firm to write him a rosier analysis of Newfoundland's financial problems.

When I came back from reporting on the war in Vietnam in the fall of 1967, a left-wing radical friend of mine gleefully claimed that the war and the riots in the United States were bringing the rich and powerful in the United States to their knees. I argued that the rich and powerful were as yet untouched, that they could not only afford to live with widespread poverty at home (50 million people), but that the war in Vietnam could be waged indefinitely and with considerable profit. I am satisfied that there is considerable evidence in what has happened since to prove me right. One has only to look at how corporate profits both in the United States and Canada have continued to rise.

Again, to quote from Gabriel Kolko's book, "The United States is today the bastion of the ancient régime of stagnation, and continued poverty for the Third World." I have lived in Africa and Pakistan and have visited South America, so I am well aware that Canadian society as a whole does not experience the poverty prevalent in what is known as the Third World. But I would argue that certain segments of Canadian society do know such poverty, and since greater and greater control of the internal workings of our nation is being exercised abroad, the likelihood that more and more Canadians will fall into this medieval abyss of poverty is a possibility that all Canadians should ponder deeply. Even at the middle levels, the lines are already being distinctly drawn. For example, in downtown Toronto there is a high-rise complex called St. James Town, inhabited predominantly by young middle-class professionals on the make. In the basement of the complex is a supermarket. On any night of the week, you can see these young middle-class workers paying for their groceries with Chargex cards and cheques. Walk a few blocks south into Cabbage Town, and the only cheques the supermarkets will accept are welfare cheques.

But let us proceed from here to a discussion of some examples of how the rich keep themselves that way and how, in acquiring their affluence, they acquire even more by selling out to even larger u.s. interests. For to do so is to come to understand much about how the poor are kept that way.

The development of the city of Toronto, like most North American cities, has been left up to a few businessmen who have bought up, in the name of free enterprise, enormous tracts of land around the outskirts of the city in the last twenty years. Through their control of real estate and capital, they constructed instant and ugly sub-divisions with a total disregard for planning or the future. Profits from land sales were considered capital gains and were therefore tax exempt; a few men made millions of dollars, and, at the same time, they created the frustrations thousands of people would live with for years to come. The taxpayers are still paying for that privilege. The remarkable fact is that all this still goes on. A few giant real-estate corporations own thousands of acres of land surrounding Toronto and the other large cities in Southern Ontario. With their grip on available land for construction, they can inflate land prices by selling properties back and forth among their subsidiaries. And with their power, they dictate terms and manipulate the governmental bodies which are supposed to regulate their activities. (For an example of this and the disastrous consequences for the poor, see Chapter 7, "Keeping the Poor That Way.") And apparently to give private land developers even more power, the government of Ontario paved the way in 1969 to provide legislation which would enable municipalities to force individuals to sell their properties to private land developers under threat of expropriation.

In the summer of 1969, one real-estate corporation, the $175-million Revenue Properties Ltd., part of the Toronto-based Rubin Corporation real-estate empire, got into trouble with the Ontario Securities Commission, and the public got a glimpse of the corporation's inner workings. It had holdings in Toronto, Montreal, and large American cities. It also had a subsidiary, Victoria Wood Development Corporation, which was a real-estate and construction developer in Etobicoke, North York, Mississauga, and Scarborough, all suburbs of Toronto. With its properties in Southern Ontario and much-publicized plans to build a satellite city outside Toronto, Revenue was also one of the Toronto Stock Exchange's most active listings. Its volume during 1968, when land prices around metropolitan Toronto rose astronomically, had been over 12.5 million shares, more than double that of any other industrial issue. When Revenue's shares were first posted on the market early in 1968, they were priced at $3; by February, 1969, they had risen to $20.87.

For most of the 7,000 share-holders, the balloon came crashing down on June 23, 1969, when the Ontario Securities Commission charged ten officers and directors, including members of the Rubin family, some of whom, it turns out, were executives of both Revenue and Victoria Wood. Most of the charges were related to what the o.s.c. alleged was information omitted from the Victoria Wood prospectus. The o.s.c. was also unhappy about Revenue's reported profits of 65 cents a share for 1968. Revenue subsequently adjusted its 1968 profits to 56 cents a share, saying that if current o.s.c. accounting practices had been in effect in 1968, the profits would have been 28 cents a share.

Revenue was allowed to continue to trade—it had been suspended from the American Stock Exchange since April— but shares plummeted to $4 by the early part of July. And on July 10, Revenue announced that it was giving a giant u.s. builder, Kaufman and Broad Inc. of Los Angeles, a one-year option on acquring control. In return, Kaufman was coming up with a $5 million note to bolster Revenue's sagging finances. The collateral was going to include mortgages on certain undeveloped properties held by Revenue and its subsidiaries—in other words, the land around Ontario cities. All that land is now mortgaged to the hilt, and Canadians are going to be a long time buying it back; if the deal goes through with Kaufman or any other American real-estate developer, the real-estate profits will all be going out of the country. Little wonder that the Toronto Real-Estate Board reported in 1969 that the price of a fifty-foot building lot in Toronto had risen from $5,000 in 1964 to $15,000 in 1969.

In September, 1969, the Ontario Securities Commission's charges against the Revenue directors and other individuals were dropped. But on October 18, Esther Cooper, sister of Alex and Harry Rubin, was tried and found guilty in provincial court of trading in Revenue securities without registration. She was fined $100 by Judge Robert Dnieper; the maximum sentence is a year in prison and a $2,000 fine. In her testimony, Mrs. Cooper revealed that during the previous November, when Revenue shares were still worth $16.50, she had sold 100,000 shares for $1,650,000. When the o.s.c. charges against Revenue officers were dismissed, there was a great outcry from Opposition M.P.'s in the provincial legislature, claiming that once again the o.s.c. had bungled the case. The o.s.c. does not have a very successful history as a watchdog agency. In an earlier case, in which Prudential Financial Corporation went bankrupt and bilked 4,500 noteholders of $17 million, it turned out that the o.s.c. had authorized the sale of stock even after the company had gone bankrupt. And when the o.s.c. charges were laid in court against the Prudential officers, they were dismissed because the wrong cabinet minister had signed the directive to prosecute. It was signed by Financial Affairs Minister Leslie Rowntree, and the court determined that it should have been signed by Attorney-General Arthur Wishart. It may have been the law, but the court's decision didn't appear to have much to do with justice.

In the spring of 1969, the furore concerning the lack of decent housing in Canada for families that made less than $8,000 a year was at its height, and government officials were belatedly recognizing that there was indeed a housing crisis. And it was just at this time that another giant real-estate corporation made a remarkable claim. Arthur Armstrong, executive vice-president of Bramalea Consolidated, a company that has held 6,000 acres of land outside Toronto for ten years, told the press that his company would realize the enormous profit of $20 million as a result of a deal made with the Ontario Housing Corporation and the municipality of Bramalea.

It seems that Armstrong could not help crowing. "This is the most astonishing real-estate transaction ever made in Canada," he said. And well it might be. The o.h.c. is a government-subsidized housing agency, and it had just paid $18,408,000 for only 1,800 acres of the 6,000-acre tract. In turn, Bramalea Consolidated would pay $11 million of this money to the municipality for providing services for 6,000 lots. Apparently this was the turning point of the deal; an independent consultant had determined the cost of servicing, not one appointed by the municipality. (There is already some question as to whether the servicing can be done for that amount.) However, this agreement absolved the Bramalea Company from the capital costs of schools and any other obligations incurred as part of the development. There were other built-in guarantees for Bramalea: 1,400 of the serviced lots would be released back to the company to sell at their own price to the public. It would profit also on the construction of half the town houses that were to be built on the development. There was also a profit to be realized on the houses that it could build on the 1,400 serviced lots returned in the deal. And there were also the surrounding 2,400 acres which the company still owned, the value of which, said company president F. B. Taylor with admirable understatement, "had major but intangible benefits which would accrue to the company because of the tremendous impact of an additional 25,000 people in the community." Even if the whole deal never goes down into the corporate text books as a masterful exercise in corporate protectionism, it is certainly a long way from the so-called open competition of "free enterprise."

Over the five years that the construction of the development will require, the o.h.c. is supposed to guarantee three- to five-bedroom town houses ranging in price from $15,000 to $17,000. It will be interesting to see if those prices hold up; when o.h.c. first got into the Bramalea area to provide "low-cost" lots for the citizens, the government agency paid $6,800 for lots it then sold for $9,800—"as a protection against speculation" was the ironic explanation. And as far back as 1953, the federal and provincial governments amassed 1,662 acres of land in the suburban municipality of Malvern at the price of $2,000 an acre; the 5,000 homes were supposed to have been ready in the fall of 1954, but fifteen years later work has not yet started on the project. And in October, 1969, Scarborough Controller Ken Morrish said that it was unlikely that services could be provided for Malvern for another five to ten years.

It is true that during 1969 the federal government made some vague attempts to regulate corporate affairs, but these were very timid steps into the corporate world. In May, Consumer and Corporate Affairs Minister Ron Basford introduced amendments to the Corporations Act. One would simply require large private companies and their subsidiaries to reveal their financial statistics to the government. Another would give the government new authority to investigate companies where fraud or serious mismanagement are suspected. To the wage-earning worker, who has to reveal fully his income every year in tax returns, it probably seems ludicrous that the government didn't already have such fundamental authority. It seems particularly shocking in light of the findings of the Watkins Report on the structure of Canadian industry, which revealed that a narrow managerial élite in this country had, through mismanagement and a lack of entrepreneurship, dissipated much of the gain from foreign business investment in Canada. This, in turn, has apparently led to even deeper foreign penetration of our economy.

But listen to the cry of pain and protest that came from the corporate world. J. W. Younger, secretary of the Steel Company of Canada Ltd. (Stelco) and head of the Canadian Manufacturers' Association, said, "The handiest Christians to throw to the lions these days are businessmen." It is amusing that Younger implies, even obliquely, that corporate enterprise is built upon the Christian ethic. More ponderously, George Williams, president of Proctor and Gamble Company of Canada Ltd., manufacturers of all that heavily advertised soap (and whose ownership rests totally in the hands of its American parent), claimed that the government threatened to indulge in legislative overkill that would drive a wedge of distrust between consumers and businessmen. The remark reveals how far Williams must be removed from the rhythms and thoughts of working-class life.

But it was Younger who, in a panel discussion with Basford on June 3, waxed with moral outrage over an amendment to the Corporations Act that would impose a maximum penalty of six months in prison or a fine of $1,000 for failure to file reports on inside stock transactions. "It is a historic concept of law," said Younger, "to punish things that are morally wrong, and leave problems of interpersonal relations to the civil courts. I observe the government relaxing penalties on such moral wrongs as homosexuality, at the same time it is imposing vicious criminal penalties [the Corporate Act amendment] for things I hardly think most people would consider wrong."

One union official of the United Steelworkers estimates

Younger's yearly earnings to be in the $100,000 bracket. Stelco made, after taxes, a profit of $67,971,231 in 1968. In the summer of 1969, Stelco faced a strike of 12,000 workers in Hamilton, as did Algoma Steel in Sault Ste. Marie. Both companies were nervously watching what settlement the International Nickel Company of Canada (Inco) would make with its 15,400 workers in Sudbury. Inco itself cleared $143 million in profit for 1968. But in their Sudbury smelter plant is a conveyor worker named Laurier Lalonde who has worked eighteen years for Inco. Before the strike, he worked fifty-five hours a week to earn $133 in take-home pay. On that he has to support his wife and two children in a city that has some of the highest living costs in Ontario. They live in an o.h.c. home, and Lalonde says they haven't been able to afford a movie in six years. His wife hasn't been able to afford new furniture for their house for the past seventeen years. I wonder what Lalonde would think of Younger's "moral" argument.

But then it seems there is evidence that the corporate executives of the mining industry have long regarded their workers as subhuman, and therefore a question of morality in this case would probably be considered inappropriate. The reluctance of the mining industry to put money back into its human resources and to provide better working conditions for its workers was pointed out early in 1969 by the Ontario Minister of Mines, Allen Lawrence. In a speech he gave to the Sudbury branch of the Canadian Institute of Mining and Metallurgy, he pointed out that although mineral products mined in Ontario during 1968 were worth $1.34 billion, making it one of the province's most important industries, colleges and universities were dropping mining courses because not enough interested students enrolled. The impression one received from Northern Ontario's mining communities, said

Lawrence, was that they were a mixture of "Dante's inferno and a London fog." Miners were generally regarded "as a cross between a man and a mole." In his speech, Lawrence told the industry's leaders to stop quibbling over working conditions. "Surely," he said, "the expense of a decent lunch-room underground is peanuts compared to the loss of time and effort on everyone's part in arguing that things are better now than ten years ago."

It seems unbelievable that in 1969 a government minister would have to tell the mining companies to fix up their lunch-rooms and stop grumbling about it, especially in an industry where the tax rides are so generous and the profits so enormous. For example, Noranda Mines Ltd. of Toronto reported in 1969 that its profits had increased over the previous year by some $3 million to $52,476,000 or $2.20 a share. It is important to remember that in Canada, the so-called public ownership of corporate stock is for the most part in the hands of about 2.9 per cent of the people who file income tax returns.

Laurier Lalonde, the Sudbury smelter worker, is represented by Local 6500 of the United Steelworkers of America. When the Carter Royal Commission on the reform of tax laws came out in February, 1967, the United Steelworkers' union was one of the few groups that made it to Ottawa to present a brief to Mitchell Sharp, then Finance Minister, urging him to accept and put into immediate practice the proposals of the Carter Report. Understandably, big business had already moved in a very big way. In the six-month period allowed, the oil companies alone had produced more than 100 briefs *against* the Carter Report.

Kenneth Carter, a fifty-five-year-old chartered account-ant with impeccable credentials, verified a fact the working man has known and lived with for a long time: that people with modest incomes were paying a disproportionate amount of income tax. "The net effect," wrote Carter, "of the whole fiscal system in Canada is a redistribution of income from those earning between $4,500 and $7,000 to those with incomes below that level," and that the one-fifth of Canadian families who earn over $12,000 a year were, by comparison, not even involved.

Of even greater interest was Carter's discovery that three particular industries, oil, mining, and life insurance, were getting away with paying a pittance. If Carter's tax reforms had been implemented immediately, industry would have been collectively paying 25 per cent more, some $532 million, in additional tax revenue to the government. This would have allowed a minimum of a 15 per cent reduction in the taxes of 46 per cent of the taxpayers. In answer to all the briefs, Sharp announced in 1967 that a White Paper on tax reform would be produced by the end of the year. But, as one reporter put it, he didn't say which year. By the summer of 1969, Parliament had recessed, and the new Finance Minister, E. J. Benson, was still making noises about "the important tax reform legislation that had to be prepared." (The watered-down version of the Carter Report, a set of delicately balanced compromises, finally appeared in the November, 1969, White Paper presented by Finance Minister Benson. It didn't hold much promise for the working poor: a married worker with two children under sixteen and an income of $6,000 a year would pay $568 income tax instead of $663. The $96 reduction would not even cover the loss in real income caused by inflation.)

In his report, Carter winkled out the most deeply entrenched economic elites and laid bare what they got away with. He showed that 1964 revenues for the insurance companies were $90 million more than expenditures, but that taxes were paid on only $5 million of that amount; total outlay to the government was $2 million. He compared this with the fact that in the same year, for the 30 per cent of their business that they did abroad, Canadian insurance companies paid $13.8 million in taxes to foreign governments. If insurance companies had been taxed according to the Carter formula in 1964, they would have paid $77 million in taxes to the federal government, an increase of $75 million.

Mining companies are given a three-year tax exemption on new mines, and oil companies have a loophole that is called a "petroleum depletion allowance." Carter showed that in 1964 more than 15 per cent of the $150 million the government relinquished under these exemptions went to eight giant mining and oil companies that had no need of this kind of government assistance.

Banks, said Carter, should also pay their own way–like other businesses–and their enormous, so-called "contingency reserves" should not be considered tax-exempt. He showed very simply that even if the banks multiplied by seven times their average losses over the past five years on loans under $500,000, they would still come nowhere near the great sums set aside as tax-exempt emergency funds. Besides, as he pointed out, there was other legislation that quite adequately protected the solvency of banks. During its October to October fiscal year of 1967-68, The Royal Bank of Canada made a profit of $35,324,403 after taxes. Nevertheless, it continued to raise its interest rates, complying with the "anti-inflation" tactics of the Trudeau government.

In the face of the findings by the Carter Royal Commission, Finance Minister Benson introduced an additional two per cent tax on all incomes, with a ceiling on the charge of $120. The only people that hurt were the ones who made less than that as a weekly wage. Benson defended his office in May, 1969, saying, "Canadians have been fortunate in having a reasonably progressive and well-administered tax system." So that "the fairness of the system could be improved," he promised proposals for tax reform in June. They didn't appear; Prime Minister Pierre Trudeau was occupied with his languages bill and an abortion law that wouldn't even touch the poor. All the while the government continued to lose tax revenues at a rate calculated to be $1,000 a minute —more than half-a-billion dollars a year.

The government, however, had appointed a ten-man Senate committee to study tax reform. It is probable that in the last days of Kenneth Carter's life—he died in the summer of 1969—he could only regard the appointments with bitter amusement. The Senate is, for the most part, the political pay-off at the end of a career. Appointments go to the dependable corporate executive who has stood by the party for years, quietly picked up the tab for those extremely expensive election campaigns, and, just as silently, doled out the money to keep the local party machinery operating. The Senate is therefore loaded with millionaires. With few exceptions, a man comes to own a million dollars in this country by inheriting enormous numbers of shares in public and private corporations, which he can then sell out to larger u.s. interests and earn even greater profit. So, quite properly, a member of the n.d.p. Opposition, Max Saltsman, rose in the House of Commons to point out the obvious conflict of interest for senators appointed to a tax reform committee, supposedly sitting to deny their own financial gain. "May I list," said Saltsman, "some of the corporate appointments of some of the senators, Mr. Speaker?"

Senator Beaubien holds appointments to Canadair Ltd., Empire Life Insurance Company—and we in the other place legislate with respect to life insurance companies—Holt, Renfrew and Company Ltd., Marshall Steel Company Ltd., Beaubien Corporation, Belding-Corticelli Ltd., Canada and Dominion Sugar Ltd., Dominion Structural Steel, London and Yorkshire Ltd., and M.G.F. Management Ltd.

Senator Cook holds directorships or appointments in the following companies: Cook, Barthel, Chelke and Martell, United Towns Electric, Dominion Buck Company, William Noseworthy Ltd., Maritime Life Assurance Company, Newfoundland Fluorspar Ltd., Great Eastern Oil Company—and it is significant to note that the Carter Report has launched a major attack against the oil industry's depletion allowances. And this Senator is a director of one of the oil companies of Canada. His other directorships are with Bank of Montreal, Colonial Cordage, and Newfoundland Brewery Ltd.

Senator Everett is the president of Royal Canadian Securities Ltd., and his other appointment is with Dominion Motors. Senator Gelinas has appointments with the Mercantile Bank of Canada, Distillers Corporation (Canada) Ltd., Canadian International Paper Company, Canadian Cement Company, John Labatt Ltd., Canadian Permanent Trust Company, Foster Wheeler Ltd., Manicouagan Power Company, Sicard Inc., Global Life Insurance Company, National Drug and Chemical Company of Canada Ltd., EMCO Ltd., Hilton of Canada, Robert Mitchell Company Ltd., and North American Holdings Ltd.

Senator Grosart is not shown, as far as I am aware, as holding any directorships. I think he ought to remain on the committee.

Senator Hayden holds appointments in the following

enterprises: The Bank of Nova Scotia, Union Carbide Canada Ltd., Rio Algom Mines Ltd., Atlantic Sugar Refineries Ltd., Acadia Atlantic Sugar Refinery Ltd., United Steel Corporation Ltd., Parker Pen Company, Allied Towers Merchants, Scotts Restaurants, Capital Wire Cloth Ltd., and Electric Finance. He holds ten other appointments as well.

Senator Laird has directorships with Western Ontario Broadcasting Corporation, International Wire and Cable Ltd., and Liquid Glaze of Canada Ltd.

Senator D'Arcy holds directorships with Canada Permanent Mortgage, Toronto and London Investment Company Ltd., Canadian Industries Ltd., Canada Permanent Trust, Consumers Gas and Triard Corporation.

Senator Thorvaldson holds directorships with Western Gypsum Products Ltd., Wesco Paints Ltd., Weshoe Industries, International Savings and Mortgage Corporation, Marshall Wells of Canada, International Laboratories, Anthes-Imperial Company, c.a.e. Industries, Canadian Premier Life, Canada Security Assurance Company, and North Canadian Trust Company.

As many people have pointed out, taxation reform is really only the beginning, and even if the federal Liberal government surprised everyone by adopting the Carter Report—and its author insisted that it had to be an all-or-nothing decision to do so—there would still be the process of redistribution, of how the money would be spent. On this, J. C. Weldon, professor of economics at McGill University, wrote in the Toronto *Star*,

One would guess that the redistribution that emerges when account is taken of defence, education, the arts,

139

highways and the rest favours people strangely like our Liberal Party. [One would hope] . . . for change to favour the old and the poor. . . . Alas, the old and the poor are less efficient politically than the upper middle class, and pay for it by enduring the Just Society that their innocence has brought upon them. In one sense, though, the penalty they pay is small. Much is wasted, but only a little is taken from the poor and given to the well-to-do.

❧ 9 ❧

Time is Running Out

You can see them standing grey and mute in the early morning bus lines, holding in one hand a lunch pail or a small brown paper bag of sandwiches. They live in the older, jerry-built suburbs put up immediately after the war, those not-yet-slums but decaying pockets you can find in Halifax, St. Boniface, and Kitsalano. They inhabit the buffer zone between the industrial wasteland and the greener suburbs, where there are picture-window bungalows on streets that are always called Pleasantvale or something like that. The kids are in school, or with grandmother, or with a neighbour down the block. The wives are those harried, unkempt women pressing shirts in the corner window of the local dry-cleaner, serving grilled cheese sandwiches in greasy burger joints, or, if they're lucky, fumbling away time and papers in the lowest echelons of municipal government. The men work at the myriad jobs in the manufacturing, construction, and service industries that are the special domain of the semi- and unskilled worker. They have, on average, a Grade Nine education, and, even if they're not yet middle-aged, they know that all the options of upward mobility are already closed to them. There are usually three or four children to support,

which is too many, because the parents earn something between $4,500 and $7,500 a year. At the bottom end of the
wage scale, they know about welfare and living on the pogey
during winter unemployment. At the upper end, they moon-
light every hour they can, because more than a quarter of
their income is gobbled up by exorbitant rents or payments on
a wooden frame house that in all probability won't last as
many years as the mortgage. There is a four-year-old car to
keep running and never enough money to swing a decent
trade-in. On average, they are $2,500 in debt to the finance
company or the bank, and both money-lending institutions
charge the highest rates possible, because, you see, they're a
"poor risk," although God knows they need the money more
than anyone else. For the majority of them, work is drudgery,
leisure time is the tube. And their life-style is that of one-third
of all families—some 7 million Canadians. They are the working poor, the lower middle class, or, to use the inhuman jargon of sociologists, "the lower socio-economic levels without
status." Caught in that no-man's land between the slums of
the inner city and the slick suburbs, their needs are ignored
because they are not poor enough to provide ammunition for
the politicians who toss around the political football that is
poverty. They are also ignored for the opposite reason; they
don't have the money or community machinery that can be
used by a politician who is seeking election. They are an
ignored and embittered class, which, at this point in our
history, neither the government nor industry could do without. They provide nearly 50 per cent of the total personal
income tax revenue. Their contributions form the largest part
of the financial pyramid that pays for the medicare and insurance programs that benefit the rich. Their slim raises are
eaten by inflation, the provincial sales taxes, and the ever-
spiralling assessment on their modest homes is based not on

what the house is worth or the owner's ability to pay, but on the cost of middle-class education, welfare, and planning policies. (In Toronto, as in many cities, it is always the lower middle-class homes that are first expropriated by the school boards.)

As industry moves into a technology where machines are replacing the men and women who now operate machines, and more is being produced with less labour, the working poor are still the stop-gap workers. As such, they are treated with contempt, the final expression of the nineteenth century master-servant relationship clung to by Canadian management. It is an attitude I heard best expressed by a young Toronto lawyer who specializes in trouble-shooting for management in labour problems. "We don't owe them anything but their hourly wage," he said. He was drinking scotch as he sat in his flossy apartment, an apartment hung with tourist trinkets brought back from holiday in Africa. He inherited his money and with it, of course, his attitudes. But for a mass-production worker in Vancouver, working hard to stay out of the unemployment lines and never taking African safaris, those attitudes are translated into a ruthless policy. "As soon as they've got a machine that can do what I'm doing half-a-cent cheaper than I can, I'm out on my ass. And there's bugger-all I, or anyone, can do."

Very few of the working poor have the protection of organized labour unions. Prime Minister Trudeau pointed this out on television in his anti-inflation speech last August, when he said, "Inflation is going to cause the greatest hardship to those living on fixed salaries and those workers in weak bargaining positions." He didn't add that those workers amount to more than two-thirds of the Canadian labour force, over 5 million workers.

From time to time, union leaders make noises about the enormous mass of workers left to fend for themselves. Michel

Chartrand, Montreal Council Chairman of the Confederation of National Trade Unions, says, "We are going to put our lawyers, union halls and other resources at the disposal of citizens' groups, tenants, and underprivileged people who lack funds to finance their fights."

But in the face of automation, the unions are having a hard enough time holding on to the membership they have. Only a little more than 2 million Canadian workers are organized in a fragmented labour structure of 475 different unions with over 9,200 locals. And two-thirds of these workers belong to unions with headquarters in the United States. In the past ten years, the union membership has avoided community problems, concentrating only on large wage gains. And in the summer of 1969, the union members on the west coast didn't even vote for socialism: they voted for the conservative, big-business policies of W. A. C. Bennett's Social Credit administration—so it is hard to believe that the unions hold any realistic ambitions about organizing and fighting for a class of workers who are soon to become confirmed discards of the technological era.

That era has not yet come to cleave the structure of society even further apart, but there is no doubt that, like a juggernaut, its development is aimed squarely at the fulcrum on which society now balances itself: the working poor, who are the pivot for poverty and wealth in our time. Bled by both sides, their days obviously numbered, it is no wonder that its members are sullen and lash out instinctively at both ends. In the swaying caboose of a freight train rolling across Northern Ontario, I once watched a bush worker steadily eye a couple of newspaper reporters from the east. Finally, full of Friday night booze, he couldn't hold it back anymore.

"What the hell are you sons of bitches doing out here writing sob stories about the goddam Indians? The Indian doesn't want to work anyway. When he's on welfare, I support him, when he's in jail, I pay for keeping him there. So why the Christ don't you write about me? I've got a wife and three kids, and I clear $72.60 a week."

The bush worker was right, of course; he pays for the welfare systems, inadequate as they are. He is also right about his alienation; nobody is really interested in him. And if he is apparently a bigot, well, he is no more a bigot than the insurance company executive who, on another Friday night, sits in the rooftop bar of the Park Plaza Hotel in Toronto and complains about "those niggers in Detroit burning down their own stores to collect the fire insurance."

The world of the working poor is dominated by the anxiety created by continual harassment from bureaucracies and their petty officials; they stand like sentinels on the borders of the world of the poor and are as frightening to deal with as any Kafka nightmare. You have to be bringing up a family of four on $4,000 a year to fully understand the sinking feeling in your stomach when one of those brown government envelopes, with its little slotted window, turns up in the mail. It may be a letter telling you that your medical insurance has been suspended for non-payment of the premium, or perhaps the Revenue Department has gone back four years to adjust its own mistake and demand that you immediately pay $83 in tax arrears.

The medical premium has been paid, of course, but it will take a long series of frustrating telephone calls, letters, and possibly visits before the department will admit its mistake. Meanwhile, doctors' bills will have been returned, and their bookkeepers will start phoning you. Everything is on the side of the bureaucracy: the interminable buck-passing to other departments, officials out for lunch, and the characteristic phrase, "Your file is not in this department," always uttered in a tone that seems to imply you therefore do not exist. For someone in a higher income bracket, such bureaucratic incompetence is only irritating, an annoyance. But for a woman trying to support a family on a budget of less than $300 a month, the temporary loss of medical insurance can be a financial disaster.

Because the minor bureaucratic officials are apparently unable to deal with the sophisticated legal manoeuvring of the wealthier middle class, they seem to justify their jobs by zeroing in on the man who is struggling to stay on his feet. An Italian immigrant in Vancouver is fined $250 for putting a porch on his house because he did not apply for an amendment to the original building permit he bought to renovate his home. Most of the houses on the same Vancouver street are owned by an absentee landlord and have been in shabby disrepair for years. The Italian has a bitter explanation for the slum landlord's apparent immunity: "He's a Canadian, I'm a lousy D.P."

In Toronto, another immigrant, Hermann Grossman, bought a rundown house on the fringes of Toronto's Cabbage Town. He thought that he would take several years to renovate it as he got the money. The house had been there for thirty-five years, given only an occasional coat of paint. But in the first two weeks after Grossman had purchased it from a trust company, no less than five different inspectors called on him with lists of repairs that had to be made or Grossman would be served with a summons for breaking city by-laws. "I replaced the plumbing, the wiring, and the heating systems," says Grossman. "I suppose I was stupid about letting them bully me into some things, but I thought this was the way they do things in this country, and I wanted to keep my nose clean. But believe me, I couldn't afford it. At the time, I badly needed the money for the small moving company I was trying to start." Grossman had to refinish the basement and pay for a new hook-up to the sewer line, but the inspectors still kept coming. Grossman says, "It was unbelievable. I would ask them, 'Look, isn't there another house in Toronto you can work over? Do you need a bribe to leave me alone?'" What infuriated him most of all was that he continually moved people in and out of homes that were in much worse condition than his own. He had two second-hand moving vans, and his rates were low. His customers were, for the most part, in the lower income brackets; often, they were on welfare. "I couldn't understand it," he says. "Here were these city inspectors at my house every week telling me I had to do this and fix that. At the same time, another city department was moving these people on welfare into houses I wouldn't put an animal to live in. I always used to ask who the landlord was. It was always a company, a real-estate developer, or a bank."

Grossman found that his second-hand trucks also made him an obvious target for police harassment. He was given tickets because his name wasn't printed clearly enough on the cab door and, on one occasion, because he had a dirty licence plate. If he went to work early in the morning, before the rush-hour traffic, his truck was always stopped and searched by police patrols looking for stolen goods. Each check would take twenty minutes. One frustrating day, it took him three hours to move seven miles across the northern section of Toronto. His truck was searched three times and given two safety checks. On this particular morning, he had left his wallet at home; he was given two summonses for not having his driver's licence. When he finally got home that night, his wife showed him a warning left by an inspector from the city health department. Apparently a neighbour had complained about his children's pet, and the health department had issued an order that Grossman's back yard be cleared of dog litter. "I went to the back window," says Grossman, "and there were two little piles of dog shit by the back fence. That's when I told my wife we were getting out." Grossman sold the house and moved out into the country, where he is now trying to start a small contracting business.

But for every alienated immigrant who is trying to make a go of it in this country and becomes convinced along the way that the bureaucracies don't want him to, there are one hundred Canadians in a similar position. Indeed, at this income level, the immigrant averages $1,000 a year more than the Canadian-born worker. In many cases, the native Canadian's bitterness is fuelled by the knowledge that, as a war veteran, he gave the best years of his life and, in many cases, his health in fighting for a society that now has nothing to share with him. The most abused ex-servicemen in this country are those Canadian soldiers who survived the battle of Hong Kong. Many of them, especially the non-commissioned ranks who spent the war in the slave-labour camps of Japan, came home broken in spirit and in health. But it wasn't until nineteen years after the war that the government finally recognized they were not "malingering ex-servicemen," but that they had the highest incidence of blindness, chronic disease, and death among all returning veterans. (Of the 1,417 survivors, more than 300 have died from diseases contracted as prisoners of war.) However, beyond that recognition, little has been done for them. The first Diefenbaker government in 1957 promised to raise veterans' pensions, which are ludicrously low. (A veteran receiving a 50 per cent disability pension, with a wife and two children to support, receives $199 a month.) The Pearson governments also promised change every year. In the summer of 1969, the Trudeau government produced a White Paper that promised the veterans a better deal. But while the veterans waited for the federal legislation, many of their spokesmen pointed out that it was too little, too late. This attitude of disregard permeates private institutions as well as the government. The attitude is: *shut up and be thankful for what you have*. When the people want a fairer deal or assistance in bettering their lot, they are made to feel like beggars.

The mass of working-class people are supposed to be satisfied with the crumbs thrown their way as they wait interminably for the middle-class liberals who run Canada to stop their intellectual posturing over reforms, the unending procession of commissions and committees, the voluminous reports by fact-finding experts, the proposals that are never acted upon—all of which are paid for by the working class. The Bilingual and Bicultural Commission cost $7,400,800, the Commission on the Status of Women, $1,750,000 so far, the Carter Report on Tax Reform cost $568,760. There is now a Commission on Canadian Communications which will no doubt spend enormous amounts of money finding out exactly what the O'Leary Commission found out in 1960.

In the Gaspé region of Quebec, sociologists and economists spent five years and a great deal of money in attempting to find out why the poor there are poor. After the research, a five-year program was started in 1968. It was labelled "a pilot project of intense social animation," and its avowed intent is apparently to have the poor learn what they already know: they are poor. It would be a good black-humour joke, except for the fact that it will cost $258.8 million, of which the federal government will pay $212.3 million. Most of the money will probably go into the pockets of middle-class experts, the professionals of poverty. Of this, Gerard Filion, a former publisher of the independent Montreal daily newspaper, *Le Devoir*, has said, "For five years we have passed a fine-tooth comb over the whole area of the lower St. Lawrence, Gaspé Peninsula, and the Magdalen Island to find out what everybody knew. . . . For a year we have been trying to implement a plan which does not include industrial development. This has been going on for six years, and we have not created a single job over the whole territory. It is time we put an end to this comedy of sociologists and economists who make plans because they don't know how to do anything else."

Related to this line of comedy is the fact that, given the opportunity, politicians and economic planners will always try to save money by paring the wages of those already working. It was such an attempt which aroused the first firm resentment of the working class against the Trudeau government's economy measures. Postmaster Eric Kierans discovered that if he could get postmen, who average about $6,200, to eat their lunches while on their daily rounds instead of returning to their postal stations, he could cut $1.8 million from his budget with the time saved. In attempting to implement this plan, Kierans turned the Post Office upside down. Workers began to work-to-rule, and the effect on mail deliveries in metropolitan areas was disastrous. In the end, Kierans had to back down publicly. To give him something to think about for the fire next time, postal workers' union officer William Houle warned that the coming fight would be over the workers' pension fund. The Post Office deducts the compulsory premiums, but the workers have no say in how their contributions are invested. The government invests the money in federal bonds with an annual yield of less than four per cent: General Motors offers 8.5 per cent on short-term bonds. It is true that this was a union-organized revolt, but the will to fight came from the employees and indicates the hardening of resistance of workers at the lower end of the wage scale. Perhaps one of the reasons it was so successful was that while Kierans was trying to save his $1.8 million, union leaders were telling the workers that the government was foregoing tax revenues of more than a half of a billion dollars, mostly from the giant corporations, because of its inability to pass tax reforms. Instead, Parliament's time was taken up with passing a languages bill that had little application to most of English-speaking Canada and Criminal Code amendments that Liberals attempted to describe as "radical," but which in fact made legal the abortions doctors were already performing. Parliament also made legal whatever consenting adult homosexuals do to each other in private and acts of bestiality committed by married couples in their bedrooms. An eighteen-year veteran of the Toronto morality squad observed that he had never in his experience heard of a married couple being prosecuted for such an offence.

If the 1969 parliamentary session seemed remote from the real problems of the working poor, the political debate was even further removed. For there was much talk about constitutional reform being the most important problem facing the nation. Unfortunately, nobody could define the problem in understandable terms.

The poor, dealing with day-to-day realities and instinctively aware that time is running out for them, sought to hear their own voice in various protest organizations. Four women on welfare founded The Just Society, a hollow laugh on the slogan which swept Trudeau to power in 1968. The Society, designed to help the poor organize among themselves, set up an office, and the first thing Bell Telephone demanded was an advance deposit of $100. Bell, the giant monopoly with assets of $2.4 billion, hastily withdrew in anticipation of bad publicity. Consumer organizations in cities across the country led boycotts of high-priced beef. And groups of women threatened to march on Ottawa when the government implied that it might cut back Family Allowance cheques in its unflagging search for economic solutions.

But these manifestations of protest were really only cries in the night. In the background, the vast superstructures of power, the economic élites and the American corporations, privately and quietly went about their profitable business. The chartered banks printed notices showing another strong increase in profits. The Royal Bank of Canada, the nation's largest bank, reported a net profit of $28.5 million for the first nine months of the year. Total revenue was reported at $488 million, up from the previous year's $384 million. And at the same time, the banks' dour business reviews forecast an unemployment rate of five per cent for the coming winter.

Meanwhile, in the summer of 1969, the cost-of-living index went over 126 points—it became 26 per cent more expensive to live than in 1961, when the index was at 100. It is obvious what this sort of inflation does to a minimum-wage worker earning $1.30 an hour in Ontario. At the same time, the government announced a freeze on the building of all low-income housing projects. In Toronto alone, 35,000 people were waiting to get into such housing. They had already waited two or three years. They would have to wait longer.

In Ottawa, the Prime Minister demonstrated his grip on the economy by going on television to announce the freezing of jobs in the civil service. He gravely informed the poor that if they didn't stop spending money, inflation would hit them hardest and that higher taxes would be the only alternative. A few days later, he left for a Mediterranean cruise. There was something incongruous about that. The day he left, I was talking to some men in a Canadian Legion Hall in Southern Ontario. They would never be able to afford a cruise on the Great Lakes, let alone the Mediterranean. They were ruefully admitting that they had voted and cheered for the Prime Minister just a year ago.

"If Trudeau called an election tomorrow would you vote for him again?" I asked.

They laughed derisively, and one man drew a finger across his throat, saying, "He's had his biscuit."

In their innocence, they voted for Trudeau, believing that he would speak for them, and now, if Trudeau has committed political suicide among the working class, who will come forward to speak for the working poor? Who will speak for the more than 2 million kids already trapped in poverty's miserable life cycle, shunted into the inferior stratas of education? Who will speak for the semi-skilled, non-union workers who are becoming the discards of automation? Who will speak for the thousands of men and women who are suddenly too old to work and are left to wait for death on a pension of $109 a month?

Will it be Senator Croll, head of the committee examining poverty, or the other wealthy law-makers on the committee? Hardly. It is just as unlikely that it will be the New Democratic Party. In the east and the west, their socialism cannot even win the confidence of the union workers. And in Manitoba, it is too soon to tell how the N.D.P. will use its slender majority. Who will fill the political vacuum? The grim answer is that there is nobody, and time is running out for the working poor.

It follows then to ask: who has given the few the right to insist that the rest of us should so undervalue ourselves? How does it become their right to demand that we should stand silently in line while injustices are imposed upon us? That we should be made to understand that a $46-million culture palace, a plaything for the wealthy, is of greater importance than children living in slums with their abandoned mothers? That a workingman cannot afford to eat beef while a millionaire is subsidized by the government to breed race horses? That the Indians are our wealthiest land-owners but the poorest of us all? That a rich man is given bail and a poor man jailed? That we should accept our old people living on dog foods while our politicians and administrators are fêted? That we should accept unemployment so that the rich may balance their books?

And when we have learned to live on their hand-outs of $28 a week, who are they to tell us we must look into ourselves after a lifetime of subjugation to discover the causes of our own poverty? Have the few learned nothing? Do they not understand that from the very beginning, as children, we were taught to deny our own value, that as we grow older, we learn that machines are more important than we are? How can they tell us to free ourselves from the pressures they have forced upon us, or to seek our equality when we know we are only pawns to be used in their game?